Kyle A. Thomas, Carol Symes
The Play about the Antichrist (Ludus de Antichristo)

Early Drama, Art, and Music

Series Editors
Katie Brokaw, University of California, Merced
Erith Jaffe-Berg, University of California, Riverside
Jenna Soleo-Shanks, University of Minnesota Duluth
Christopher Swift, New York City College of Technology
Andrew Walker White, George Mason University

Kyle A. Thomas, Carol Symes

The Play about the Antichrist (Ludus de Antichristo)

A Dramaturgical Analysis,
Historical Commentary, and Latin Edition
with a New English Verse Translation

DE GRUYTER

ISBN 978-1-5015-1798-3
e-ISBN (PDF) 978-1-5015-1357-2
e-ISBN (EPUB) 978-1-5015-1341-1

Library of Congress Control Number: 2023935167

Bibliographic information published by the Deutsche Nationalbibliothek
The Deutsche Nationalbibliothek lists this publication in the Deutsche Nationalbibliografie;
detailed bibliographic data are available on the internet at http://dnb.dnb.de.

© 2023 Walter de Gruyter GmbH, Berlin/Boston
Cover image: © The British Library Board, Source: Add. MS 11695 f143r
Printing and binding: CPI books GmbH, Leck

www.degruyter.com

Contents

Foreword —— VII

Acknowledgments —— VIII

List of Illustrations —— X

Abbreviations —— X

Part I: **The Play: Historical, Literary, and Performance Contexts**
(Kyle A. Thomas)

Introduction —— 3

1   A Performance Dramaturgy —— 6

2   History, Eschatology, and Education: Contextual Frameworks for *The Play about the Antichrist* —— 24

3   Liturgies, Æsthetics, and Symbolic Meaning-Making —— 44

Part II: **A New Translation and Edition**
(Kyle A. Thomas, Carol Symes)

Introduction —— 61

Dramatis Personæ —— 67

Ludus de Antichristo (edited by Kyle A. Thomas) /
The Play about the Antichrist (translated by Carol Symes) —— **70/71**

Bibliography —— 153

Foreword

In the early stages of undertaking a doctoral dissertation on *The Play about the Antichrist*, I approached my advisor, Carol Symes, about the need to investigate the multiple dimensions of this twelfth-century text through its performance for a twenty-first-century audience: the sources of its dramatic affect from moment to moment; the sense of rhythm, tempo, and pacing that can emerge only in performance; the ways in which the movement of bodies captures and propels the arc of the story and its characters' trajectories; its environmental and atmospheric effects on the performance space; and, most importantly, where and how the play meets the audience in the course of performance. When her fresh verse translation was staged on the campus of the University of Illinois at Urbana-Champaign (on 19–20 April, 2013), I was most notably struck by the ways and places in which the audience seemed most engaged with the performance, adding to it their empathy, their energy, and their excitement. Carol's translation did much to ensure the success of that production and spurred wider conversations about the need for actor- and student-friendly performance translations of medieval Latin and vernacular plays. My commentary on the play and diplomatic edition of its manuscript text—which accompany her translation—are the result of those initiatives.

This new approach to *The Play about the Antichrist* and its historical and performative contexts represents the culmination of research that I pursued from 2010 to 2018, when I completed a doctoral dissertation entitled "The *Ludus de Antichristo* and the Making of a Monastic Theatre: Imperial Politics and Performance at the Abbey of Tegernsee 1000–1200." Preparing this volume has been an opportunity to refocus much of that research, in order to make the play accessible to a wider audience and to facilitate its future performance, and so to forge closer connections between those who study medieval theatre and the contemporary theatre practitioners who can make it come alive in new ways. Plays like *Ludus de Antichristo* hold a great deal of potential when enacted and reinvigorated, teaching us more about the medieval milieus from which they arose and showing us how they can continue to resonate with fresh audiences.

March 2023　　　　　　　　　　　　　　　　　　　　　　　　　　　　Kyle A. Thomas

Acknowledgments

The fully-staged premier of this translation by Carol Symes was funded by the Andrew W. Mellon Foundation and produced in conjunction with the symposium on "Performing the Middle Ages" at the University of Illinois at Urbana-Champaign in April, 2013. The authors wish to thank the Program in Medieval Studies at the University of Illinois, especially its director at the time, Professor Charles D. Wright, and all who were involved in the production: Julia Celentano (assistant director), Amanda Williams (scenic designer), Zeke Hafenrichter (technical director), Jess Gersz (costume coordinator), Bradford Chapin (co-sound designer), and Yu-Yun Hsieh (co-sound designer); as well as the actors: Ninos Baba, Tarice Baxter, Stephen A. Bruce, Jasper Booth-Hodges, Jesse Chen, Cheyenne C. Drew, Mark E. Fox, Mateo Hurtado, Josephine Lane, S. Negar Tabibian, Taylor Toms, Ehsan Totoni, and Elana Weiner-Kaplow.

We also thank the Department of Theatre at the University of Illinois and the faculty who supported the research undergirding this commentary: Professors Jeffrey Eric Jenkins, Tom Mitchell, J. W. Morrissette, Valerie Robinson, and Robert G. Anderson. Their kindness and support helped fuel Kyle's passion for medieval theatre and enabled him to contribute to the work of the department's top-notch artistic and scholarly community. Special thanks are due to the members of Kyle's interdisciplinary dissertation committee: Professors Martin Camargo, Lofton Durham (Western Michigan University), Andrea Stevens, and Katherine Syer. It is also imperative to acknowledge the debt to Scott Holsclaw for introducing Kyle to Bertolt Brecht during his undergraduate studies, and for supporting his interest in Brecht's theories.

Our primal debt is that owed to Eckehard P. Simon, Victor S. Thomas Professor of Germanic Languages and Literatures, Emeritus, at Harvard University. Born in 1939, in the medieval town of Schneidemühl-Piła (now Poland, then in West Prussia), Professor Simon survived the firebombing of Dresden as a child and, in 1955, emigrated to New York with his mother and sisters. He graduated *summa cum laude* from Columbia College in 1960 and completed his PhD at Harvard in 1964, under the direction of Joachim Bumke. His early work on the *Minnesänger* Neidhart von Reuental, among other courtly poets, was followed by two landmark studies in medieval theatre history: *The Theatre of Medieval Europe* (1991), a state-of-the-art overview for researchers, still an invaluable resource; and a monumental archival study of secular German plays, *Die Anfänge des weltlichen deutschen Schauspiels, 1370–1530: Untersuchung und Dokumentation* (2003). At Harvard, where he taught from 1964 until his retirement in 2009, he was a dearly loved teacher, introducing thousands of undergraduates to the joys of medieval literature and theatre in his two popular courses, "The Medieval Court" and "The Medieval Stage." Both were enlivened by his passion for the material, his self-deprecating humor, and his beautifully curated slides (in an age before PowerPoint, these were truly innovative).

Eckehard Simon inspired countless graduate students in many fields of medieval studies, training them generously in his own teaching and research methods. Carol was first introduced to the *Ludus de Antichristo*, and to the study of medieval theatre, as one of his Teaching Fellows in 1994. Since then, she has done her best to pass along what she learned from this beloved Doktorvater to her own Doktorkinder—among whom Kyle gratefully counts himself. We both mourn his death on 2 May, 2020, when he fell victim to the COVID-19 pandemic at the age of 81.

Carol Symes
Kyle A. Thomas

List of Illustrations

Figure 1: Folio page on which the *Ludus de Antichristo* begins (near the bottom of column A).
Figure 2: A scene from the production of *The Play about the Antichrist* at the University of Illinois in Urbana-Champaign, 2013.
Figure 3: A scene from the production of *The Play about the Antichrist* at the University of Illinois in Urbana-Champaign, 2013.
Map 1: A map of pertinent locations of cites and monasteries in twelfth-century Europe.
Figure 4: A diagram of one possible scenic layout for the *Ludus de Antichristo* based upon the dimensions of the St. Quirinus Church at Tegernsee Abbey.
Figure 5: Folio containing roughly seventy lines from the beginning of the *Ludus de Antichristo*, preserved in a late twelfth-century manuscript from St. Georgenberg Abbey.
Figure 6: The *Firmetur manus tua* liturgical setting from the eleventh-century Anderson Pontifical.
Figure 7: The *Firmetur manus tua* liturgical setting from the eleventh-century Sherborne Pontifical.

Abbreviations

MGH *Monumenta Germaniae Historica*
  – Ldl: *Libelli de lite imperatorum et pontificum*
  – Briefe d. dt. Kaiserzeit: *Die Briefe der deutschen Kaiserzeit*
  – DD O II/O III: *Die Urkunden der deutschen Könige und Kaiser, Otto II und Otto III*
  – Epp. sel.: *Epistolae selectae*
  – SS rer. Germ. [N.S.]: *Scriptores rerum Germanicarum* [*Nova series*]
BnF Bibliothèque nationale de France, Paris
BSb Bayerische Staatsbibliothek, München

Part I: **The Play: Historical, Literary, and Performance Contexts**

Introduction

The play commonly known as the *Ludus de Antichristo* (*The Play about the Antichrist*) is one of the most unique and exciting examples of medieval drama to come down to us. It features major geopolitical conflicts, popular themes of Latin Christian eschatology, both localized and universal liturgical traditions, propagandized characters, and pedagogical materials for medieval monastic instruction. It was composed around 1159 at the imperial Benedictine abbey of Tegernsee, in the independent German duchy of Bavaria, within what Frederick Barbarossa (r. 1155–1190) had dubbed "the Holy Roman Empire" just two years earlier. It survives in a single manuscript copied at that monastery between 1176 and 1186. Occupying five parchment leaves and not including a title, it was bound up with a variety of other materials and is now in Munich's Bayerische Staatsbibliothek (Bavarian State Library), where it is shelfmarked Clm (Codex latinus monacensis) 19411.

This faithful and engaging new verse translation of the *Ludus de Antichristo* is designed to facilitate both future performance and enhanced appreciation of the play and its medieval milieu. By replicating the rhyme schemes and meters of the Latin original, and by restoring the texts of the liturgical chants whose *incipits* were abbreviated in the manuscript, it achieves what no other translation—or edition— has even attempted.[1] The accompanying commentary, meanwhile, returns the play to the political events, ongoing debates, and specific monastic community from which it emerged. No previous analysis of the play in any language has accomplished these twinned and inseparable goals.[2] Analyzing the documents of medieval drama—even those texts that seem obviously identifiable as plays—is difficult precisely because the relationship between text and performance functions differently, even inversely, to what is expected of scripted drama in the modern era.[3] Moreover, it is necessary to view any performance as embedded within its historical and documentary contexts while, at the same time, seeking to recover the dramaturgical foundation that supported its staging.

---

[1] Karl Young, for example, was unaware of the existence of the *Alto consilio* conductus: *The Drama of the Medieval Church*, II:373, n. 1. And although he supplied citations for other liturgical elements, he did not reproduce them.

[2] The first, by William H. Hulme, was published in 1925 under the title "Antichrist and Adam." The second, more often cited and widely used as a teaching text, is *The Play of Antichrist*, translated by John Wright in 1967. Neither is consistently accurate, and Wright's is often misleading or erroneous: see the notes to the translation.

[3] Symes, "The Medieval Archive," 32; and Symes, "Liturgical Texts and Performance Practices," 241–44. See also Schechner, *Performance Theory*, 66–111.

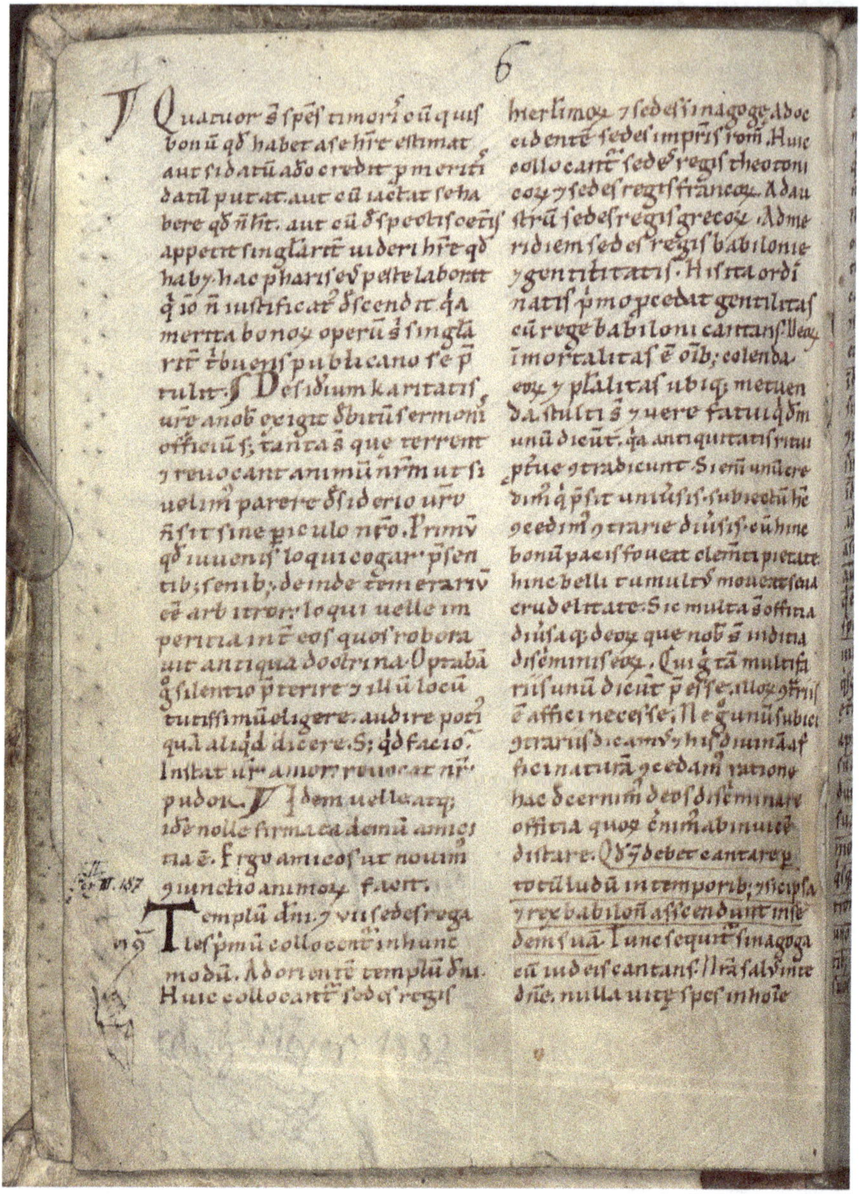

Figure 1: The opening rubric of the play is indicated by a manicule in the left-hand margin of the extant manuscript. Munich, Bayerische Staatsbibliothek Clm 19411, fol. 2va.

As a multifaceted, expertly crafted work of theatre, the *Ludus de Antichristo* enacts the anxieties, expectations, and convictions emanating from the community at Tegernsee. At the same time, precisely because it is both masterfully made and specifically located, it also proves an excellent vehicle through which to explore affective parallels with our world today, inviting us to reconsider our place within and connection to our own communities. For both of these reasons, we need to understand the political, eschatological, and educational agendas behind its creation at Tegernsee Abbey in a specific historical moment; we also need to understand how and why the text of the play was eventually included within its extant manuscript, in order to further the educational and diplomatic objectives of the monastery and its fellow Benedictine communities. Explaining these circumstances and contexts is the task of Chapter 2. In Chapter 3, we will further examine the deeply encoded æsthetic and dramatic vocabularies that imbued the original performance(s) of the play with special significance for its target audiences, through its re-use of liturgical elements. Together, these two chapters are also intended to advance the creative imperative introduced in this first chapter: the bridging of medieval and postmedieval or (post)modern theatrical traditions in order to recover the former's significance while simultaneously revealing its renewed relevance for our own apocalyptic moment.

Chapter 1
A Performance Dramaturgy

The Play about the Antichrist opens with an unusually detailed description of the scenographic requirements and organization of the space for performance.[4] According to these directions, seven individual *sedes*, prominent "seats" or thrones, are arranged in the space according to the cardinal directions. Each seat represents one of the various kingdoms in the play, and the allegorically conceived regnal characters who embody the authority of each kingdom operate from these respective positions.

Gentilitas—the female allegorical character representing pagan "Gentiles"—enters first, accompanied by the King of Babylon: a representation of the resurgent Abbasid Caliph al-Muqtafi, whose army had repulsed an attack on Baghdad by the Seljuq Turks in 1157, just two years before the play's scripting. Gentilitas opens with a monologue which, like the rest of the play's verse dialogue, is explicitly described as being sung, rather than spoken. She introduces both the underlying pedagogical aims that inform the play's dramaturgy, thereby functioning as a kind of prologue, as well as her own character's command of logical and rhetorical argumentation. Citing the incongruities of nature as the basis for her polytheistic cosmography, she belittles the Christian belief in a singular, yet tripartite, God.

> If we believed [God] singular
> in all the universe,
> then we'd believe his actions are
> contrary and diverse. (p. 71, 18–22)

After this, Gentilitas ascends to join the King of Babylon at his seat. At this point, Synagoga—the symbolic representation of Judaism—enters wearing a veil over her eyes and explains her disbelief in Christ as the salvific Emmanuel. She also expresses her distrust of Christians who would believe in a man capable of raising the dead and yet unable to save himself from crucifixion.

Both Gentilitas and Synagoga thus present different but parallel perspectives that cast doubt on Christian theology. And yet, the audience of the play would have been trained to recognize that theirs are weak rhetorical positions, built more upon fanciful language and emotional reasoning than on authoritative truth: disputational *faux pas* designed to elevate the significance Ecclesia's forthcoming entrance.

---

[4] On the scripting and manuscript layouts typical of medieval dramatic texts, see Symes, "The Appearance of Early Vernacular Plays" and "The Medieval Archive and the History of Theatre."

Figure 2: Synagoga (wearing a veil) speaks to the audience with Ecclesia on the platform behind her. University of Illinois production in Urbana-Champaign, 2013. Photo Credit: Kyle A. Thomas.

In this way, the play introduces its dramatic arc from the outset as an eschatological *Heilsgeschichte* or "holy history";[5] a world constructed in seven stations, visually and historically complete, awaiting with anticipation the triumphal entrance of Christianity on the world stage.

The description of Ecclesia's entrance thus lifts the tone to one of pageantry. Dressed in a crown and breastplate, flanked by the characters of Mercy and Justice, and followed by the Emperor (representing the Holy Roman Emperor, the title assumed by Fredrick Barbarossa in 1157, two years before the play's composition) and Apostolicus (a diminutive and derogatory allegorical depiction of the Pope), the allegorical figure of the Church leads her retinue into the space while singing a festive processional liturgy known as the *Alto consilio* (p. 75, 4 ff.). The significance

---

5 Eschatology, or the theological exploration of those events and symbols at the Biblical end of days, was a common vehicle through which to express critiques of society, culture, politics, and religious practices during the Middle Ages. See Petry, "Three Medieval Chroniclers."

of this *conductus*, and all the other liturgical elements of the play, will be discussed at greater length in Chapter 3. Here, it is important to note that this song was so well known to the play's community that neither its text nor its accompanying notation were included in the script. Once the procession is complete, Ecclesia ascends to her throne, accompanied by Apostolicus, while the Emperor takes his place upon his own throne. Then the rest of the regnal characters—the King of the Franks, the King of the Greeks (that is, the Emperor of Byzantium: here given an insultingly lesser title), and the King of Jerusalem (a reference to the Crusader state established in 1099)—make their entrances and take up their positions in the performance space as designated by the opening stage directions.

The action of the play then shifts to the Emperor. Under his interpretation of Roman imperial purview, reinforced by historical precedent, he declares his intention to bring all the world under his dominion. His imperial eye lands first on the Kingdom of the Franks. He thus engages the abilities of the Imperial Ambassadors to facilitate formal interactions with the King of the Franks and other states represented in the drama. Displaying their command of the rhetorical and oratorical arts, the Imperial Ambassadors deliver the Emperor's decree in respectful terms, while emphasizing the authority of their lord's imperial might. Unmoved, the King of the Franks rejects the demand of imperial fealty, prompting the Emperor to declare war against him. The text reads, "And immediately, he shall rally his battalions to assault the King of the Franks, who comes out opposing him and who will be led back to the seat of the Emperor as a captive" (p. 87, 27–29). After the King of the Franks swears fealty to the Emperor, the action and dialogue repeats, with the Imperial Ambassadors delivering the same demand to the King of the Greeks and the King of Jerusalem, but without resistance from either king, who have evidently witnessed the defeat of the Frankish king and learned their lessons.

With the Christian kingdoms now united under the ægis of the Holy Roman Empire, the King of Babylon lays siege to Jerusalem in order to eradicate Christianity's hold over the city. Underscoring once again the importance of emissaries in carrying out the action of the plot, the King of Jerusalem sends his Royal Messengers to the Emperor to request his help in lifting the siege. Answering the call, the Emperor and his army prepare to do battle with the King of Babylon, urged on by an Angel who appears to deliver the message that his forces will be victorious. The Angel leads the assemblage in the liturgical antiphon *Judaea et Jerusalem nolite timere* (Judea and Jerusalem, fear not)—typically reserved for Christmas Eve and, again, so well known that its text is not included in the script (p. 103, 13–20). After the King of Babylon's defeat, the Emperor lays his imperial scepter and regalia at the altar in Jerusalem, signaling an end to the eschatological trajectory of his imperial aims. From this point forward, the Emperor's identity is subsumed into that of the King of the Teutons.

Figure 3: The Angel delivers the message *Judea et Jerusalem nolite timere* before the Emperor rescues the King of Jerusalem. University of Illinois production in Urbana-Champaign, 2013. Photo Credit: Kyle A. Thomas.

Having reached the mid-point of the play, the dramatic action follows the exploits of Antichrist until the end. Once the King of the Teutons returns to his throne, the Hypocrites enter and begin to "gain the good will of the laity" (p. 105, 17), eventually making their way to the *sedes* of the King of Jerusalem. The stage directions mention that the King of Jerusalem welcomes the Hyprocrites and accepts their counsel. At this point, Antichrist enters accompanied by the allegorical characters of Hypocrisy and Heresy. It is also explicitly instructed that he should wear a breastplate hidden under his garments (p. 105, 20). Similar to the Emperor's earlier declaration, Antichrist shares with Hypocrisy and Heresy his plan to pronounce himself Christ and, in doing so, bring the world under his dominion. In response, the Hypocrites sing verses from a Psalm included in contemporary coronation ceremonies: another familiar liturgical element whose text is not given in the manuscript (p. 109, 26ff.).

Antichrist's plan begins with the deposition of the King of Jerusalem, who immediately goes to the King of the Teutons to express his outrage at Antichrist's ignominious treatment. Meanwhile, Antichrist and the Hypocrites turn to the Temple, where Ecclesia has remained since she accompanied the Emperor to Jerusalem, and they subject her to "many insults and beatings" (p. 111, 20) forcing her to retreat back to her throne and to stand with Apostolicus. Antichrist thus mirrors, in reverse, the earlier actions of the Emperor by enacting his campaign to bring the world kingdoms under his subjection. Sending out the Hypocrites as his ambassadors to the King of the Greeks, he orders the king swear fealty to him. The Hypocrites deliver Antichrist's demands with all of the forcefulness and none of the diplomacy displayed earlier by the Imperial Ambassadors. Nevertheless, the king swiftly concedes, kneeling before Antichrist and offering up his crown. Antichrist then marks his forehead with "the first letter of his name," an A (p. 115, 10–11). This sequence is repeated with the King of the Franks, except that the demands delivered by the Hypocrites are also accompanied by gifts—presumably to flatter the king and induce his speedy capitulation.

But the King of the Teutons is not as easily swayed. He rejects the gifts brought by the Hypocrites and so Antichrist, in frustration, responds by amassing an army from among his new vassal kings. When the ensuing battle does not go in Antichrist's favor, he changes tactics: he begins to perform a series of healing "miracles"—meta-theatrical moments in which, as the text directs, it should be made clear to the audience that those being healed of their ailments are merely acting. These dumb shows culminate with Antichrist resurrecting a man "pretending to have been killed in battle" (p. 127, 28). The King of the Teutons, whose piety allows him to be duped by these false miracles, is thus persuaded and swears his loyalty to Antichrist. Upon seeing the growing power of Antichrist, both Gentilitas and the King of Babylon follow suit, and also swear fealty to him.

With the world's powers subdued, Antichrist turns to converting the faithful, beginning with Synagoga. The Hypocrites successfully convince her that Antichrist is the prophesied Messiah and, like the kings before her, she takes the mark of Antichrist on her forehead. But the Old Testament prophets, Enoch and Elijah, appear to show Synagoga the error of her judgment. Through their exhortation, she realizes that Antichrist has deceived her and she removes her veil. Embittered, the Hyprocrites deliver the news of the prophets' "blasphemy" to Antichrist (p. 143, 29), who then demands to have all three brought to him for judgment. When they resist, Antichrist has them taken off and killed. With little else to stand in his way, he prepares to have the entire world gather before him and worship him. Upon the completion of his self-elegy, there is a cacophonous sound and Antichrist is struck dead. Ecclesia closes out the play with a liturgical chant (*Laudem dicite Deo nostro*, "Speak praise to our God") from the Feast of All Saints (1 November). Like the other liturgical elements featured in the play, this one is not fully scripted (p. 151, 24–30).

Altogether, the plot is driven by the tensions that arise amongst and between temporal and spiritual powers, framed by eschatological events commonly associated with the end of days in the theology of Latin Christianity. This is perhaps most palpable in the final moments of the play when, climactically, Synagoga is misled by Antichrist only to find herself martyred for finally converting to belief in (a false) Christ. The drama is bookended by statements of belief, mostly from Ecclesia, while the rest of the plot revolves around parallel but opposing actions performed by its two central figures, the Emperor/King of the Teutons and Antichrist. The ending collapses the epic quality of the drama into a small moment shared between Ecclesia and all those gathered together in the space. The affect thus sets the mood for expectation of the Second Coming. While the text of the play does not necessarily make for the most exciting read, the plot is a carefully designed platform for communicating important political and pedagogical messages that are made more apparent in performance.

Dramaturgical Methodology

In April of 2013, Carol Symes's rhymed verse translation of *The Play about the Antichrist* was first staged on the campus of the University of Illinois at Urbana-Champaign, as part of a symposium on "Performing the Middle Ages." The principal aims of the production were to investigate how to navigate the needs of a relatively large cast and the demands of an outdoor performance space, as well as to explore the ways in which the play could engage and entertain a twenty-first-century audience. Although there were no overt attempts to re-create the conditions of performance in mid-twelfth-century Tegernsee, the process of moving the play from the page to the stage nevertheless resulted in the adoption of strategies that revealed some foundational aspects of how the medieval dramatic artifact could translate into modern performance. The following dramaturgical analysis is intended to encourage future productions that may wish to capture the medieval spirit of the original while freeing up space for practitioners' own creative spirits, agendas, and æsthetics.

As Cathy Turner and Synne K. Behrndt explain, dramaturgy is the critical, analytical, and practical evaluation of the relationship between drama and performance. When examining historical scripts, in particular, dramaturgy utilizes techniques that allow for both literary (that is, scholarly) and interpretative (that is, practicable) readings and realizations of a given text. Dramaturgical thinking especially requires "contextual analysis where the performance is considered as a part of a wider network of meaning."[6] This interdependency of practice and research aims to reveal a play's points of engagement with imagined audiences—whether medieval or modern, scholarly or artistic. Thus, excavating a play's dramaturgical roots in community connectedness enables exploration of the ways that it engaged contemporary (historical) practitioners and audiences without constricting the creative potentials of those who might wish to interpret the play for *their* particular communities in the future.

In the twelfth century, *The Play about the Antichrist* enabled embodied engagement with the larger political, ecclesiastical, ritual, and eschatological circumstances surrounding the interconnected world of Tegernsee Abbey. Mobilizing the performative framework of their lived experiences, the monks of that particular Benedictine community, building on the security of an identity inculcated by generations of established educational and liturgical practices, dramatically translated their perspective on the world as a means of exercising agency over events beyond their immediate control. *The Play about the Antichrist* must be understood as play—not just *a* play—designed to carve out space, time, and ritual from the prescribed performances of life under monastic rule in the twelfth century. As the performance studies scholar, Richard Schechner, explains: "play and ritual are complementary," enabling and "inverting accepted procedures and hierarchies" on their way to connecting meaning to particular activities and procedures.[7] Though the circumstances, inspirations, and sources that inform the structure and shape of *The Play about the Antichrist* strike us as intently serious, we need to be curious about the lighthearted, even mischievous, moments that shine through in performance. The play's eschatological and apocalyptic tonalities are constantly balanced by levity and playfulness, as in the exaggerated gesticulating of the Hypocrites as they attempt to influence the "laity" with their pious affectations, or in the "winks" to the audience during the sequence of blatantly false miracles, or even the ridicule written into Apostolicus's diminutive status. Working with the play in the collaborative process of performance leaves little doubt that moments of humor and satire were purposeful—and effective—aspects of the drama.

Indeed, the Latin term *ludus* (play, game) was a nineteenth-century designation, and thus should be understood as a scholarly "reading into" the document's status as a work of drama. And while an investigation into taxonomic distinctions

---

6 Turner and Behrndt, *Dramaturgy and Performance*, 35–36 at 36.
7 Schechner, *The Future of Ritual*, 26–27.

is beyond the scope of the present work,[8] this particular play certainly reflects the playfulness that was a feature of the community from which it emerged. Froumund of Tegernsee (ca. 960–1008), the famous schoolmaster of the abbey, wrote of favoring dramatic, and even comic, teaching aids in the monastery's *schola*, explaining that exaggerated gestures, over-the-top expressions, wild movements, dancing, and musical interpretations of material were all effective means of engaging his pupils.[9] Froumund relied on performance and entertainment in his teaching so as to better inculcate those concepts and skills he believed most valuable to monastic education. Furthermore, there are descriptions of games, including the medieval mathematical board game known as Rithmomachia, accompanying the play in its surviving manuscript. Thus, it is no stretch to imagine that *The Play about the Antichrist* would rely on the same entertaining theatricality as a means to effectively extend and exert its messages across a network of individuals and communities familiar with—or specifically trained in—those same instructional methods.

Theatrical Modality and Audience Engagement

That a performance would treat the impending apocalypse with playful humor seemingly belies our perception of the medieval world's devotion to practices that we designate as "religious" today. But rather than attempt to relay a mimetically realistic affect grounded in the play's twelfth-century Christian beliefs and rituals, it is important that any future performance consider how the category "religious" serves as a vehicle for transmitting the concerns and conflicts of the play and its performed frameworks. In his *Short Organum on Theatre*, Bertolt Brecht explains that our modernity—and the corresponding phenomenon that is our theatre and its conventions—obscures what is truly happening through the interactions of premodern theatre, and thus "restricts our pleasure" in such plays.[10] As the most influential dramaturgical theorist of the twentieth century, Brecht was critical of theatrical conventions born from a reliance on Aristotelian definitions of dramatic efficacy. He even placed significant emphasis on didacticism in his own dramatic practice, borrowing from his medieval antecedents (especially the morality

---

8 On the scholarly discourse surrounding taxonomic descriptions of medieval literature and their value for critical and historical analyses of medieval drama, see Clopper, *Drama, Play, and Game*; Dox, *The Idea of Theater*; and Kelly, *Ideas and Forms*. On how modalities of engagement like playfulness transcend genre and classification in medieval literature, see Thomas, "Playful Performance."
9 Symes, "Performance and Preservation," 36.
10 Brecht, "A Short Organum on the Theatre," in *Brecht on Theatre*, 179–208 at 183.

plays) to achieve "a theatre of ideas."[11] As such, Brecht proves an excellent guide for moving toward a mimesis that navigates premodern conventions such as the absence of proscenium framing, the need to decode once-familiar rituals and conventions, and—importantly—maintains an emphasis on facilitating a pleasurable performance experience: a consideration that is often lacking in modern theatrical treatments of medieval plays. We must therefore interrogate the modality of performance, the nature of character, and the æsthetic distance (or lack thereof) we find in this particular example of medieval drama.

The characters, situations, and actions of *The Play about the Antichrist* operate in allegorical modes that tie their representational functions to the theological and ontological conditions of twelfth-century Christendom, as seen from the perspective of the Tegernsee community. Allegorical representation was a common medieval idiom and æsthetic that could express complexities of spirituality, temporality, and perception for a particular community, or audience, equipped to unpack their meaning.[12] Furthermore, the spheres of public discourse created by ongoing ideological conflicts, such as the Investiture Controversy, became sites wherein "the unsayable (*apophasis*) becomes the sayable (*kataphasis*) through the language of allegory."[13] Much of *Antichrist* operates in the mode of *allegoria in factis*, representing contemporary events and individuals placed in "conversation" with a well-established eschatology, so that the historical necessity of monasticism is not only symbolized, but demanded.[14] Embodied by and for the monks of Tegernsee and other Benedictine houses of Bavaria, performance facilitates intersection with the coded meanings in the text so as to enliven and make real the visuality signaled in the allegories of the text. The bodies of the performers give new symbolic meanings to the allegorical modalities of those texts from which it draws. The viewer is meant to *see* monasticism at the center of allegorical meaning in the play.

With monasticism at the dramatic center of meaning-making in the play, the liturgical elements included in the play work to enhance the *allegoria in factis* for the targeted audience, replaying ritual as a familiar act of transformation and interaction between performing body and symbolic actions and things, but enhancing or upending its "proper" or acceptable meanings. This approach to theatricality was

---

11 See Potter, *The English Morality Play*, 241–45.
12 Akbari, *Seeing through the Veil*, 8–10.
13 Kobialka, *This Is My Body*, 172.
14 The medieval concept of *allegoria in factis* was laid out in the eighth century by the Venerable Bede in *Libri II: De arte metrica et De schematibus et tropis*. Much of the conceptual framework for *allegoria in factis* as applied here to *The Play about the Antichrist* is borrowed from Kobialka, *This Is My Body*, 173, and his assessment of Hildegard of Bingen's *Scvias*, which contains the *Ordo Virtutum* (*Service of the Virtues*)—a play contemporaneous to *Antichrist*.

seemingly well understood by Brecht when, defining aspects of the estrangement effect (*Verfremdungseffekt*), he explained how acting must take into consideration and engage what the audience considers to be "socially important." For Brecht, the actor must perform "in such a way that nearly every sentence could be followed by a verdict of the audience and practically every gesture is submitted for the public's approval."[15] *The Play about the Antichrist*—and medieval drama more broadly—feels so different from our theatrical sensibilities because, as articulated in Brecht's critique of modern acting techniques, it is the *becoming* of character rather than the *being* of character that is the source of meaning.

Following a Brechtian approach to *The Play about the Antichrist* provides production strategies that help (post)modern audiences and performers, familiar with character portrayals that follow the conventions of theatrical Realism and acting techniques stemming from Stanislavski's System, navigate meaning-making by interrogating character, action, and dialogue—rather than relying on empathic connection to the *ethos* or the inner monologue (*dianoia*) of a character and the their individual motivations. While a medieval audience would have found in the play meaningful associations with the rituals and representations of monastic knowledge, a modern audience will seek out specific implications of the humanity behind the allegories. Therefore, just as the medieval ritual unpacked significance as a transformative act, any performance today must look to the space between the actor and the character—the act of *becoming* the character—as a way to provide an anchor of humanity, a contemporary source of meaning, that can be instructive and meaningful for an audience today.

In the 2013 production, this approach was employed in the character portrayal of Synagoga—an effectively anti-Semitic allegory and, together with Ecclesia, one half of a common medieval visual motif that was meant to signify Christianity triumphant.[16] The actress playing Synagoga discovered moments in the performance when she would lift her veil—a medieval signification of the Jews' collective blindness to Christ as the Messiah—and, showing her discomfort or distaste for the representation she was undertaking, present her disaffected state as a point of empathic engagement with the audience. This distinction between the actress and Synagoga allowed for moral commentary on the character's position within the drama and enabled a negotiation between the medieval representation of Judaism and the postmodern recognition of the dangers of such a representation. In essence, Brecht guides us toward performance that enables an experience with "the medieval," but

---

15 Brecht, "Alienation Effects in Chinese Acting," in *Brecht on Theatre*, 95.
16 See Rowe, *The Jew, the Cathedral and the Medieval City*, especially Chapter 2, "Ecclesia and Synagoga: The Life of a Motif," 40–80; and Cohen, "*Synagoga conversa*," 309–11.

not via an attempt at "authenticity." This parallels the effort made by the extant text to reach twelfth-century audiences capable of understanding the meanings behind its allegorical interpretations of contemporary events, rituals, and rhetoric.[17]

Synagoga is arguably the most dynamic character of the play, transforming from a common medieval allegory for Jewish unbelief to the embodiment of theological fortitude against the enemies of Christendom, as identified in Christian eschatological narratives: a character arc that Jeremy Cohen identifies as *Synagoga conversa* ("Synagoga converted"). Cohen's analysis of Honorious Augustodunensis's twelfth-century treatise on the Biblical Song of Songs posits that Honorius "transformed the converted Synagoga into the veritable vanguard of Christ's church in its struggle against Antichrist and the forces of evil."[18] This dramatic deviation from the more pervasive belief in Jewish collusion *with* Antichrist, much like the deviations made by the play's adaptation of familiar liturgies, would have served to reveal Synagoga as acting under the inspiration of Honorius's exegetical and allegorical construction of Jewish transformation. Thus, any performance of the play today must take into account the functionally anti-Semitic framing of Synagoga in the drama, while also considering how to treat her as a symbolic representation of hopeful change and redemption in the midst of an ever-intensifying global eschaton.

Therefore, the approach to the character in performance must dedicate mimetic space to social commentary as a means to enact the character's transformative arc. The differentiation between character and actor, foundational to Brecht's estrangement effect, bifurcates the mimesis of the actor's performance into that which seeks to represent the medieval and that which presents the means toward transformation, thereby facilitating a discursive space and inviting the audience into it. "The attitude [the actor] adopts is a socially critical one [... such that] performance becomes a discussion (about social conditions) with the audience."[19] Brecht's approach is equally applicable to every other character in the play, with each actor contributing their "socially critical" perspective to their character's actions, dialogue, potential for transformation, and capacity for inspiring

---

[17] The awareness of actor as distinct from character is a feature of premodern theatre and served to draw attention to this relationship as a critical commentary in performance: see Soule, *Actor as Anti-Character*; and Aronson-Lehavi, *Street Scenes*.

[18] Cohen, *"Synagoga conversa,"* 310. A twelfth-century copy of Honorius's exegesis on the Song of Songs, *Exposito in Cantica canticorum*, was produced at Tegernsee and is extant in Munich, Bayerische Staatsbibliothek (hereinafter BSb) Clm 18125. Furthermore, both Clm 18125 and its sister copy from the nearby monastery of Benediktbeuern, BSb Clm 4550, both indicate a wider circulation of Honorius's exegetical works in Bavaria during the twelfth century.

[19] Brecht, "Short Description of a New Technique of Acting," in *Brecht on Theatre*, 139.

empathy. The unbridgeable temporality between ourselves and the medieval world is, as Brecht exclaims, "alienated [i.e. estranged] from us by" the distance of time,[20] making any attempt to achieve a sense of the Real from the perspective of the medieval, or to portray an allegorical character through the techniques of psychological Realism a problematic and, frankly, futile endeavor.

Performance Space and the World of the Play

The play's opening description begins with the words *Templum domini*, indicating that the following manuscript text, and the play in performance, unfold in relation to the "Temple of the Lord." This *didascalia* directs that seven *sedes regales* ("royal seats") are to be set up before the beginning of the play, arranged according to the four cardinal directions, with the Temple of the Lord in the East (*ad orientem*). *Templum domini* establishes a mimetic ecclesiastical demarcation within the world of the play—whether or not it was, or is, staged in a church. It therefore occupies the same space as the traditional location of the church's altar and, as such, the focal point of the dramatic landscape within the world of the play, as within medieval Christendom.

In its attention to the arrangement of spatial signifiers, then, the play obviously relies on the stagecraft and æsthetics of contemporary liturgical performance. The royal seats of both the King of Jerusalem and of Synagoga, which are arranged around (*collocantur*) the Temple of the Lord, visually establish a relationship to one another in much the same way as a diptych upon an ecclesiastical altar.[21] United in composition with the Temple of the Lord, they reflect the sacro-political worldview of Latin Christianity. Additionally, the liturgical function of the altar as the site of salvific sacrifice, perpetually re-enacted in the Mass, lends particular significance to certain moments of the play: Ecclesia and the Emperor offering up the imperial crown, Hypocrisy and Heresy crowning Antichrist, Synagoga's conversion, and Ecclesia's final pronouncement and invitation to "Praise our God" in song.[22]

The other royal *sedes* correspond to geographical locations associated with an allegorical figurehead who symbolizes authority over that part of the world. Each *sedes* is a "seat of power" and also features a lordly seat, like the *cathedra* of

---

20 Brecht, "Short Description," in *Brecht on Theatre*, 140.
21 This is in accordance with Kroesen's functional definition of medieval altarpieces in "The Altar and its Decorations in Medieval Churches," 155. Dronke also refers to two St. Nicholas plays from Hildesheim as a "diptych" in *Nine Medieval Latin Plays*, xix.
22 See Kieckhefer, *Theology in Stone*, 64–70.

a bishop or princely throne: indeed, the play uses a Latinized form of the Greek term *thronos* (*tronus*). This was another staple of medieval liturgical stagecraft: for example, the eleventh-century *Officium stelle* (Office of the Star) from nearby Freising opens with a choral narration which explains that "the king should ascend and sit on his throne" (*ascendat rex et sedeat in solio*: here using the more conventional Latin term). It was also a staple of Frederick's own imperial *mise-en-scène*. The *Annales Cremonenses* (Annals of Cremona, from 1189) describe how, upon his reception into that allied city during his Italian campaign of 1159 (the very year of our play) he had a "great *platea*" (*platea maior*), a dais or raised platform, built in the center of the city on which he "sat in splendor" (*magnifice sedit*) to receive his subjects. As Hendrik Dey shows, enactment of imperial authority was expressed in visually significant and material forms that could "designate the arena where the most characteristic and symbolically pregnant interactions between governors and governed unfolded."[23]

Furthermore, the stagecraft for the world of the play reflects the educational conventions of Tegernsee, to be discussed in Chapter 2, as well as the shifting political, ecclesiastical, and eschatological landscape of twelfth-century Europe which the monks had to navigate. For example, the text's location of the royal seat for the King of the Greeks *ad austrum* ("toward the south wind") was borrowed from compass wind charts and maps which had been commonly taught in *scholae* since late antiquity, metaphorically imbuing the world with divine meaning.[24] In this cosmography, "winds act as direct agents of God, carrying out his will, sometimes as messengers."[25] While the royal seats and their allegorically embodied authorities are fixed into place, the projection and transmission of authority are effected by the various messengers and ambassadors who, mirroring the winds, have the real agency. The royal seats are elevated and command vertical space, but the moving messengers master horizontal space, drawing the eyes of the audience with them and enabling direct interactions. This immersive and multi-dimensional theatre experience is at once strikingly postmodern and truly medieval in its mimetic construction of the monastery as "the setting for learning" and a place where "love of

---

[23] Dey, "From 'Street' to 'Piazza'," 939.
[24] See Marchitello, "Political Maps: The Production of Cartography and Chorography in Early Modern England," 13–40 at 18. The connection between drama and instructional charts is further attested by Universitätsbibliothek Erlangen-Nürnberg, MS 391, which is an eleventh- or twelfth-century collection of comedies by the Roman playwright Terence and contains (on fol. 1r) a diagram of the quadrivium and a compass wind chart. On Tegernsee as the possible origin of the manuscript, see Thomas, "The *Ludus de Antichristo* and the Making of a Monastic Theatre," 186–87.
[25] Obrist, "Wind Diagrams and Medieval Cosmology," 76.

one's fellow man is less a series of actions than an emotion, a psychological event, a stage in the individual's progress toward God."[26]

Performing a Network (in the Twelfth and Twenty-First Centuries)

The Play about the Antichrist was one monastic community's immediate response to social, political, and ecclesiastical changes in the mid-twelfth century. The resulting drama is a carefully wrought tapestry of tropes, narratives, representations, traditions, rituals, and ideas designed for an audience who would know how to read its meanings: both a physical audience present in performance(s) but also a network of further-flung interlocutors who may have experienced it by report, or even in textual form. One of these was the community at St. Georgenberg Abbey in the Tyrol, founded in 1138, which possessed at least a partial copy of the play.[27] Since the early eleventh century, Tegernsee had cultivated and enjoyed a wide reputation as a center of learning and literary output which had resulted in long-lasting connections to many Benedictine houses in Bavaria, and well beyond. It was no insignificant outpost on a distant frontier, nor was it disconnected from the wider network of European political and ecclesiastical elites—especially during the reign of Emperor Frederick.

The treatises, letters, and other texts that were bound together with *The Play about the Antichrist* in its sole complete manuscript show that it continued to function as an instructional model for effective diplomatic and disputation skills long after Frederick had died—not unlike his dramatic avatar—on crusade, in an attempt to recapture Jerusalem from the forces of the great sultan Ṣalāḥ ad-Dīn (Saladin, r. 1174–1193) in 1189.[28] As will be discussed in Chapter 2, the play provides examples of oratory, commentaries on power and authority, and perspectives on the rhetoric of diplomacy and epistolary form. In this sense, it was not unlike

---

26 Walker, *Docere Verbo et Exemplo*, 117–19 at 118.
27 This copy now consists of a seventy-line fragment, Fiecht, Stiftsbibliothek, MS 169, vol. 4, fol. 39v: see Figure 5. See Riedmann, "Ein Neuaufgefundenes Bruchstück des *Ludus de Antichristo*," 16–38. Given that the St. Georgenberg community relocated to the city of Fiecht in 1708 (it returned to the original site in 2019), and given that unbound quires used for instruction or performance rarely survive intact, there is every reason to suppose that this manuscript was once complete. Whether or not it was copied at Tegernsee is unclear. See also below.
28 On the ubiquity of the works sharing the same manuscript as the play, and their influence in developing a medieval dispositional network and culture, see Novikoff, *Medieval Culture of Disputation*, 67.

the increasingly popular dialogic commentaries on certain authors and texts that were circulating among scholastic circles: the *Dialogus super auctores* (Dialogue on Authors) by Conrad of Hirsau, the *Didascalicon de studio legendi* (Collected Teachings on the Study of Reading) by Hugh of St. Victor, the several commentaries of Adelard of Bath, and many other twelfth-century examples. *The Play about the Antichrist* takes the mimetic theatricality of the dialogic narrative and fully stages it, while its surviving manuscript contains many of the very educational works recommended by these influential teachers, particularly for use within monastic environments.[29] *Antichrist*, as both performance and script, therefore dramatizes not only the instructional texts that were found in the cloister school at Tegernsee, but what could be learned from them. The play was a participant in a lively network of communities that shared the contents of their libraries and the strategies of their curricula, thereby advertising Tegernsee's special "brand" and the cultural capital it had accumulated.

As disputations over prevailing contemporary issues trafficked in and out of the monastery, the play created a map—a dramatic *mappa mundi*—for navigating the larger networks within which Tegernsee was in dynamic interaction. Though a full discussion is beyond the scope of the present work, the play should be further appreciated for its representations of the spatial intersection between individual and communal monastic agencies and the broader exchange of ideas unfolding on the landscape of European political and ecclesiastical reform. In particular, this conception of monasticism was influenced by conversations concerning not only the relationship between secular and sacred authorities (at the heart of the ongoing Investiture Controversy) but also contemporary debates regarding the nature of the Real Presence of Christ in the Eucharist and its significance. While the sacramental terms and spiritual stakes of this Eucharistic Controversy are deeply complex—even for medieval scholars and theologians today—one of the crucial points of disputation was the relationship between a sign/symbol and its referent, a debate which proved influential on other systems of representation beyond the Eucharist.[30] In that vein, Tegernsee's *Antichrist* both described and enacted that

---

29 Many of those authors and the works on which they comment are discussed in Novikoff, *Medieval Culture of Disputation*. See also Mews, "Monastic Educational Culture Revisited," 182–97; and Whitbread, "Conrad of Hirsau as Literary Critic," 234–45.
30 See Bedos-Rezak, *When Ego Was Imago*, 102–7, for an excellent analysis of how the scholastic debate at the heart of the Eucharist Controversy influenced documentary practices and the interpretation of sign-referent systems like seals. Kobialka, *This Is My Body*, 101–45, places this discussion of Eucharistic theology into conversation with the developments and interpretations of medieval liturgical drama happening concurrently in the extant record. On "Eucharist Semiotics," see Zysk, *Shadow and Substance*, especially Chapter 1.

abbey's engagement with these larger issues while, at the same time, deploying the text of the play as an emissary operating within its wider twelfth-century network, appropriating well-known liturgical practices alongside specific representational conceptions of monasticism in order to assert the monastery's most authentic or "real presence" within that network.

It is therefore necessary to consider how any performance of *The Play about the Antichrist* might work to simultaneously represent, critique, and *intervene in* matters most pertinent to a given society. In its own context, the dramatic action of the play worked to express and enact the monastic agency of Tegernsee within the network formed during performance. So, for example, the 2013 production sought to incorporate social media into the performance as a twenty-first-century analogue for the broader interactions and interventions of the original play. Here, Serge Moscovici's concept of "social representations" may prove instructive. Moscovici, a social psychologist, conceives of social representation as a more focused yet fluid understanding of Émile Durkheim's theory of collective representations, suggesting that social representations work "to familiarize ourselves with the unfamiliar." These representations are effected "through a degree of consensus among [community] members," in which the individual makes "implicit negotiations in the course of conversations" regarding the community's "symbolic models, images, and shared values," in order to develop a common language that gives meaning to the everyday interactions within the community.[31] What makes social media a particularly apt extension of medieval theatricality is its combination of visual and textual representations that both capture and promote collective opinion, or enable its critique (for example, retweets, memes). Moreover, the aims of social media are largely affective, seeking to frame representations in a way that ties emotion to response.[32]

Thus, *The Play about the Antichrist* provides many future opportunities for devising a symbolic language that is accessible to an interactive audience. The allegorical characters, setting, stagecraft, costumes, props, music, and rituals could all be adapted to comment on issues of pressing concern in any place or time. The 2013 production created a social media hashtag, #WhoWillYouFollow, to draw attention to the power of individual and collective agency, and the necessity for accountability, in the political culture and public institutions of the United States at that time. In the end, the issues at the heart of the play and scripted into its dramatic narrative—its appropriation of eschatological themes, its promulgation of affective language and

---

31 Moscovici, *Social Representations*, 149–52.
32 See the concept of emotional anchoring in social representation theory discussed in Höijer, "Social Representations Theory," 8–9.

imagery, its æsthetic frameworks and rituals, even its emphasis on edification and community—all transform the abstractions of contested ideology into enactable, useful modes of instruction and entertainment delivered via the most effective medium: participatory performance. By finding social representations that speak to contemporary problems, the play is capable of reaching into the space created by social media to unite the instructional and/or affective nature of its representations in order to engage an audience and, more, to create a community.

Reflections on the Future Possibilities of Medieval Drama

The Play about the Antichrist is a deceptively simple drama. The plot is relatively straightforward and repetitive, its characters are not emotionally or psychologically complex, it requires no great spectacles nor special effects, and it seems bound to a very specific medieval context that could not be replicated elsewhere. Of course, this seeming simplicity is a result of modern misunderstandings of medieval drama, writ large, as well as the relative neglect of this particular dramatic artifact. But a theatrical staging of this play (and, indeed, many other medieval plays) is an invitation to the imagination, as well as to a deeper understanding of medieval drama's power and potential. One need not be a historian of theatre nor a scholar of the Middle Ages to enjoy the play or to see in it great potential for an engaging, entertaining—even paradigm-shifting and immersive—theatrical experience. In addition to offering this new introduction to the play, and a commentary on its historical context and liturgical elements, the goal of this work is to spark new interest in medieval drama as a creative platform on which to build a future theatre that is also unmoored from the conventions of the proscenium arch, the æsthetics of psychological Realism, and an Aristotelean model of theatrical efficacy.

The possibilities for medieval plays, and perhaps especially for *The Play about the Antichrist*, are quite limitless in the twenty-first century. Few other historical eras produced dramatic artifacts of such theatricality that transform space, place, person, and perception through performance. Undeniably, *Antichrist* is playable today in any number of traditional theatre settings or found spaces; it can be produced by amateur and professional companies alike; it can be staged for live audiences or creatively adapted for online and streaming platforms; its æsthetic can amplify a strong medieval "flavor" or reflect new fashions and trends. Most importantly, *The Play about the Antichrist* is especially advantageous as a dramatic medium through which to excavate and explore the conditions and circumstances of human interaction, by employing creative theatrical parallels in performance. It is hoped that these chapters will spark many more possible approaches to the actor- and audience-friendly translation of the play that follows.

Moreover, such approaches to *The Play about the Antichrist* are equally applicable to productions of other medieval plays. The temporal distance between ourselves and these plays—particularly the very many medieval Latin dramas that have seldom been translated with performers in mind—can make it difficult to forge a connection with them. Nonetheless, we know that some of these dramatic texts survive because they were composed and received with dramatic intentions, and for audiences capable of deciphering those intentions; when "intentionalities coincide—not accidentally, but deliberately for the sake of representation—we are in the presence of a theater," as Jody Enders puts it.[33] But *we* were never the *intended* audience for this, or any, medieval play. The intentions of *Antichrist* do not *coincide* with us so much as *collide* with our world and perspectives. Such collisions may produce, at best ineffectual or, at worst, negatively affectual responses that result from significant shifts in the sentiments, *mores*, and expectations of postmedieval, (post)modern audiences.

This is why Brecht's theory of the estrangement effect is so helpful: the play, as a work of a bygone world, is already unusual to us and performance is an opportunity to work with an audience, creating a common experience and collective understanding. In essence, it is the reverse of the process that Brecht describes: we must take the dramatic artifact and, through performance, draw attention to its "peculiarity" in our world, thereby establishing a point from which we can better know *what this world of ours is* and *how we may better live together in it*.[34] Performing medieval drama becomes a collaborative excavation of those intentions that have been hidden away from us by time. We may never find them, but that is not the point. We can enjoy and be educated by the process of "digging up" the phenomena that shape the drama and take meaning from our shared moments of discovery and awe.

---

33 Enders, *Murder by Accident*, 123–24.
34 See Brecht, "Short Description," in *Brecht on Theatre*, 143–45.

Chapter 2
History, Eschatology, and Education: Contextual Frameworks for *The Play about the Antichrist*

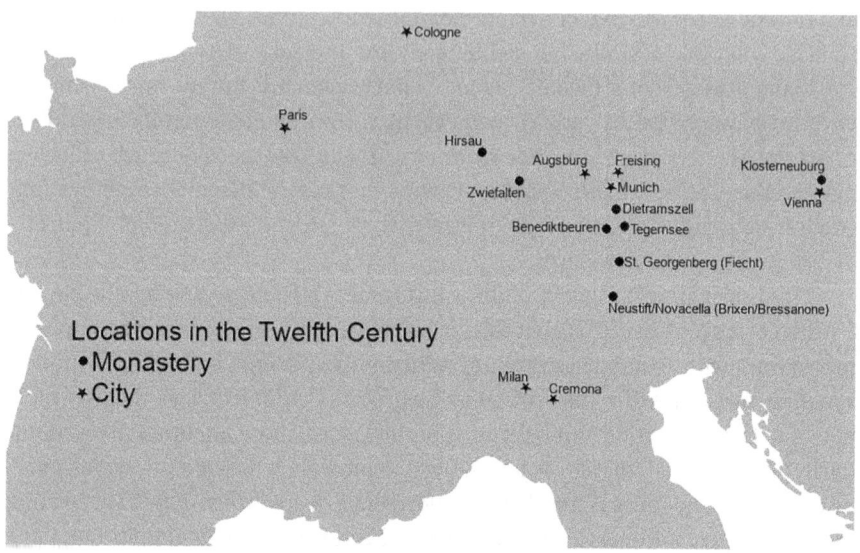

Map 1: Map of pertinent locations in twelfth-century Europe (Credit: Kyle A. Thomas).

In 1717, not long after setting out to collect and document the many medieval manuscripts preserved in the Benedictine monasteries of Bavaria, the Austrian Benedictine and historian Bernhard Pez (1683–1735) came upon the library at the abbey of Tegernsee—nestled in the foothills of the German alps, some thirty-five miles south of Munich. It is easy to imagine Pez carefully examining its many important manuscripts before he eventually turned to an unassuming "little codex"[35] containing histories, letter formulas, rhetorical treatises, and copies of correspondence from the abbey's medieval past. Within this tiny miscellany, and taking up only a few pages in it, he came upon a section that opened with instructions detailing how to

---

[35] Gisela Vollmann-Profe, *Ludus de Antichristo*, I, first used this diminutive yet affectionate term to describe the codex, just 16cm by 11.5cm (6.25 x 4.25 inches)—small enough to be a literal "handbook." Unless otherwise specified, translations from Latin and German in this section are by Thomas.

set up a space for the performance of a play. Pez must have found this text unique because he included a full edition of it in the second volume of his *Thesaurus Anecdotorum Novissimus* (1721), entitling it *Ludus Paschalis de adventu et interitu Antichristi* (The Easter Play about the Rise and Fall of the Antichrist).

Pez's publication of the *Ludus* and the manuscript's subsequent removal to the Bibliotheca Regia Monacensis (Royal Monastic Library)—now part of the Bayerische Staatsbibliothek in Munich—ensured its survival for posterity and brought the play to the attention of future scholars. By the early nineteenth-century, amongst a growing interest in the literary artifacts of German history and the increasing lure of pan-Germanism,[36] the play was celebrated for its political and eschatological themes; its connection to the poetic and scholastic traditions of Tegernsee; its evidence of the liturgical and theological innovations of German monastic communities; and its dramatization of the imperial ambitions of Frederick I "Barbarossa," the self-styled Holy Roman Emperor.[37] Indeed, the well-respected Professor of Theology at Erlangen University, Gerhard von Zezschwitz, proclaimed that, upon reading it, one "immediately recognizes that the ideas and powers dominating all imperial and ecclesiastical life of that time are gathered together here, as in a burning mirror, and reflected in a camera obscura before the spectator."[38]

Though few scholars disputed the political agenda of the play and its allusions to Emperor Frederick, there remained questions regarding its association with the Easter liturgy in which Pez had placed it. In 1868, Heinrich Reidt argued that it was more likely to have been a literary exercise rather than a drama, stripping it of any place within the liturgical calendar and renaming it the *Ludus de Antichristo*.[39] Reidt thus brought into greater focus the question of its liturgical setting and the reasons for its inclusion of specific liturgical elements, all of which remained crucial to its examination by German scholars in the latter part of the nineteenth century and into the twentieth.[40] Meanwhile, the two seminal Anglophone studies of medieval drama from the early twentieth century came to opposite conclusions. E. K. Chambers, in *The Mediæval Stage*, claimed that it "was almost certainly performed at Advent";[41] while Karl Young, in *The Drama of the Medieval Church*, argued

---

36 Crane, *Collecting and Historical Consciousness*, 5–6.
37 See Kugler, "De Werinhero, sæculi XII. monacho Tegernseensi"; Engelhardt, *Dies memoriae Jesu Christi vitae restituti pie celebrandos*; and von Zezschwitz, *Vom römischen Kaisertum deutscher Nation*.
38 von Zezschwitz, *Vom römischen Kaisertum deutscher Nation*, 87.
39 Reidt, *Das geistliche Schauspiel*, 24–44 at 37.
40 See Froning, *Das Drama des Mittelalters*, I; Gundlach, *Heldenlieder der deutschen Kaiserzeit*, III; Wilhelm Meyer, "Der Ludus de Antichristo"; and Reuschel, *Die deutschen Weltgerichtsspiele*.
41 Chambers, *The Mediaeval Stage*, II:62–63.

that its descriptions of liturgical elements "do not establish it as related directly to the services of the Church."[42] While divergent, both opinions reflect the reductive, Darwinian hypothesis that early medieval drama must have evolved from liturgical tropes and their ritual enactments during the ninth and tenth centuries.[43] But why would a play derived from a well-known eschatological narrative[44] seemingly foreground political partisanship over the monastic call to liturgical labor, the *opus Dei* of St. Benedict's sixth-century *Rule*? This question continues to thwart scholarly efforts to understand the relationship between the play's highly politicized message and its use of pre-existing liturgical materials, or to locate the occasions on, and setting in, which it would have been enacted.

Despite more recent research, the *Ludus de Antichristo* continues to defy attempts at classification within the wider canon of medieval drama and remains marginalized in the study of early European theatre. And yet the *Ludus* is perhaps the most significant surviving example of the critical role that theatre played in the political, educational, and spiritual work of medieval monastic institutions. When returned to its performative and manuscript contexts, the play reveals how one monastery navigated a turbulent period of reform within the Roman Church and its long-simmering tensions with the Holy Roman Emperor.[45] Indeed, the play stands as a visible and vocal witness to a wider public sphere in which monasteries, princely courts, and local communities negotiated the stakes of political and spiritual authority through performance. Therefore, the *Ludus de Antichristo*, like any play, cannot be understood without accounting for its enactment. Bernhard Pez helped to ensure the survival and notoriety of its extant text, but there now remains the necessary imperative that first precipitated the play's preservation on parchment.

---

42 Young, *Drama of the Medieval Church*, II:394.
43 See Hardison, *Christian Rite and Christian Drama*, Essay II: "The Mass as Sacred Drama," 35–79; also Dox, *The Idea of Theater*, Chapter Two: "Transmission and Transformation: Liturgical Allegory and the Idea of Theater," 43–71.
44 The events and characters of the play follow closely the tenth-century *Epistola Adsonis ad Gerbergam reginam de ortu et tempore antichristi* (Adso's Letter to Queen Gerberga Concerning the Advent and Time of the Antichrist) by Adso of Montier-en-Der. See McGinn, *Apocalyptic Spirituality*, 89–96.
45 This historiographical approach to the documentary practices of early medieval plays is more fully articulated in Thomas, "The Medieval Space."

Dramatizing the Apocalyptic Narrative of Medieval Christian Eschatology

The medieval drama which has come to be called *The Play about the Antichrist* is the extant script of a performance that emerged from a highly charged environment of symbolic communication, ritual practices, community politics, and public debates that framed a received account of apocalyptic events. The primary source from which the plot was adapted, around 1159,[46] is the "Letter from Adso to Queen Gerberga Concerning the Origin and Time of the Antichrist" (*Epistola Adsonis ad Gerbergam reginam de ortu et tempore antichristi*), written in the tenth century by the Benedictine monk Adso of Montier-en-Der (d. 992).[47] This open letter—a common medieval medium—was to become one of the most well-known treatises on the actors, events, and portents that would precede the Second Coming of Christ, and it would shape medieval eschatological theories and inspire a multitude of apocalyptic narratives and artworks from the tenth through the thirteenth centuries.

One of the most prominent of these was the eleventh-century *Book of Flowers* (*Liber Floridus*, literally "Blooming Book") by Lambert of Saint-Omer, which contains a history of the world and includes a narrative of apocalyptic events taken mostly from Adso's letter. Like this earlier work, *The Play about the Antichrist* is a relatively faithful re-telling of Adso's eschatological sequence: the circumstances that would precipitate the entrance of the Antichrist into the world and his destructive efforts to deceive the faithful peoples, kingdoms, and institutions of Christendom. It is also important to note that, like later twelfth-century editions of the *Book of Flowers*, *The Play about the Antichrist* couples this apocalyptic plot with a medieval map of the world—a *mappa mundi*—in the form of its dramatic *mise-en-scène*, which is described in the detailed instructions for staging that are a significant part of the play's text.[48] Not only was the legacy of Adso's treatise far-reaching and long-lasting, it is clear that, by the twelfth century, there was an established docu-

---

46 According to the paleographical analysis of Plechl, "Die Tegernseer Handschrift," 419, much of the contents of the codex were collected before 1178, during the abbacy of Rupert of Neuburg-Falkenstein. The dating of the play to around 1159 is based on Plechl's analysis ("Die Tegernseer Handschrift," 460) and on its clear relationship to the increased efforts through which Tegernsee Abbey sought to strengthen its ties to a new bishop in Freising and a new advocate (*vogt*) named to oversee matters pertaining to the abbey's authority over its daughter cloister at Diestramszell. These circumstances are discussed further in the section "Playing Identity Politics."
47 Adso of Montier-en-Der, "Letter on the Origin and Time of the Antichrist," 89–96.
48 The earliest extant copy of a *Liber Floridus* manuscript that contains a *mappa mundi* is Ghent, Universiteitsbibliotheek, MS 92, fol. 241r.

mentary culture that coupled visual and geographic symbolism with the eschatological narrative of the letter—a culture that helps to contextualize the important ways in which *The Play about the Antichrist* could intervene in the shifting political landscape of medieval Europe.

It is obvious that the monk(s) who created this imaginative apocalyptic drama found contemporary significance in the nearly two-century-old letter. Indeed, Adso's description of the Antichrist as a "minister of Satan" (*minister Satanae*), an agent acting on behalf of his diabolical lord, was directly relevant to the deteriorating relations between earthly ministers who served the two most powerful institutions of medieval Europe: the Papal See and the Holy Roman Empire.[49] In the tumultuous decades of the Investiture Controversy, which began in the latter half of the eleventh century and continued well into the twelfth, the administration of ecclesiastical oversight and the legal and historical sources of political authority were subject to constant debate. This ongoing controversy placed many intersecting communities—lay, monastic, and clerical—in the middle of the struggle for power and supremacy, while also threatening the fragile unity of Latin Christendom. Moreover, the customs, rhetorical conventions, and ritual protocols that had long shaped the interactions of secular and ecclesiastical elites were being displaced by the increasing formality of administrative courts populated by a new clerical class of influential bureaucrats.[50]

In this climate, the play's Antichrist is figured as infiltrating and subverting the established institutions of the medieval world—a representation which resonated with Benedictine monastic communities like Tegernsee, whose traditional roles were now being challenged and usurped by the secular clergy and by newer monastic orders like the Cluniacs and Cistercians. For centuries, these more established houses had educated young men—both novices and nobles—in the mastery of documentary practices, rhetorical excellence, courtly conduct, and diplomacy. This explains why the play's many ambassadors place such a strong emphasis on the knowledge of history and the long-standing precedents that undergird the exercise of the Holy Roman Emperor's imperial authority in the global politics of Christendom. Indeed, Adso's eschatological narrative was predicated on a perception of history and Biblical exegesis in which the past was constantly being realized in ongoing events, revealing their significance as they unfolded. History's translation of the past into the present also imbued the liturgical performances, documents,

---

49 Ziolkowski, "Cultures of Authority," 438–39.
50 See Reynolds, *Kingdoms and Communities*, 42–59, for an assessment of the shifts in documentary practices that evidence the other exchange that occurred during this period. See also Melve, *Inventing the Public Sphere*.

and traditions produced by monastic communities, in turn constituting specific markers of identity and proofs of authority.[51]

But Adso was not the only eschatological source from which the dramatists drew inspiration in reframing the political tensions. Frederick's uncle and biographer, Bishop Otto of Freising (1114–1158), crafted a similar apocalyptic narrative in his *Chronica sive Historia de duabus civitatibus* (Chronicle, or History of the Two Cities) that deviates from Adso's letter in one important way. In Otto's interpretation, the Roman Empire is not embodied in the authority of the King of the Franks, as in Adso's letter—which, after all, was addressed to Queen Gerberga as the wife of King Louis IV (r. 936–954). Rather, Otto explains that many of his contemporaries (and, indeed, himself) interpret the eschatological role of the Roman Empire to be realized in the intertwined relationship of Empire and its protection of the Holy See in his own day.[52] In other words, the power and might of the Roman Empire's legacy was not only represented by the authority of the Imperial Crown, but the papacy's subjugation to it. (Needless to say, the authenticity and eschatology of the Roman Empire was a broadly contested point under Frederick, who styled himself as "Holy Roman Emperor" in opposition to Emperor Manuel I Komnenos and the Roman Empire of Byzantium—represented in the *Ludus* as "the Kingdom of the Greeks.") It is not difficult to see whence Otto's conception of political and sacred authority emerged, and how his sentiments shaped the treatment of the diminutive character of Apostolicus in the play. Indeed, given the shifting geopolitical landscape, it is likely that German imperial apologists were moved to revisit and revise Adso's narrative precisely because they wanted to make it clear that "the King of the Franks"—at that time, the pious but hapless Louis VII (r. 1137–1180)—had yielded any former imperial claims to "the King of the Teutons."

For the monks of Tegernsee, in the middle of the twelfth century, Adso's letter and Otto's eschatology were thus read together as prefiguring the developments that were taking place in their own world: a perception that was not unique to Tegernsee. In his treatise "On the Search for the Antichrist" (*De investigatione Antichristi*), the influential theologian and teacher Gerhoh of Reichersberg (1093–1169) condemned theatrical games (*ludi*) and spectacles featuring "men who disfigure themselves in the guise of demons" (*homines se in demonum larvas transfigurant*) as evidence of the deep corruption being wrought by the Antichrist in the world.[53]

---

51 See Harvey, "Continuity, Authority and the Place of Heritage," 47–59. On the way in which medieval legal authority was a product of this historicity, see Clanchy, "Medieval Mentalities," 83–94.
52 Otto of Freising, *The Two Cities*, 458.
53 Gerhoh of Reichersberg, *De investigatione Antichristi*, 315–16. See also Clopper, *Drama, Play, and Game*, 43–47.

Gerhoh accordingly frames the demonic actor as a minister performing the wishes of a diabolical master subverting the Church, and thereby signaling the beginning of the end-times. By contrast, in *The Play about the Antichrist*, the Old Testament prophets Enoch and Elijah—who also feature in Adso's letter—are cast as eschatological ministers who confront the Antichrist and urge the audience to reject him and return to faith in Christ as the end approaches. They finally manage to convert the character of Synagoga, representing the Jewish community which would collectively convert prior to the Second Coming.[54] In their different ways, then, Gerhoh's treatise and *The Play about the Antichrist* are participants in a medieval milieu in which dramatic performance was a uniquely potent—and, for Gerhoh, dangerous—vehicle for eschatological interpretations of current events in which ministers played significant roles.

But not all aspects of the play's plot were taken from Adso or Otto. The allegorical characters of Ecclesia (the Church) and Synagoga were borrowed from the Pseudo-Augustinian "Debate of Ecclesia and Synagoga" (*Altercatio Ecclesiae et Synagogae*): a fifth-century dialogue that dramatizes the legal, historical, and theological arguments in support of their respective rights to worldly authority. A popular text throughout the Middle Ages, it is extant in a ninth-century manuscript which was likely produced at Tegernsee and which must have influenced the playwright(s) of *Antichrist*,[55] who "harnesses a patently theological discourse over the scriptural and historical relationship between Christianity and Judaism and reformulates it as a contest with worldwide consequences."[56] While it is important to note that Synagoga's character is undoubtedly framed by the anti-Semitic rhetoric of Latin Christendom, the play treats Synagoga as a misguided but sympathetic figure whose execution at the hands of Antichrist's ministers is meant to shock and sadden the audience, even as it exemplifies the Antichrist's successful demolition of ecclesiastical institutions.

---

[54] On the dramatic construction of Enoch and Elijah and their relationship with Synagoga as a participant in wider conversations regarding Jewishness and Christian eschatology, see Cohen, "*Synagoga conversa*," 330–31.

[55] Staatsbibliothek zu Berlin, Preußischer Kulturbesitz MS Theol. lat. oct. 157. See Izydorczyk, *Manuscripts of the Evangelium Nicodemi*, 21–22.

[56] Rowe, *The Jew, the Cathedral*, 49–54 at 54.

Playing Identity Politics: Propaganda and the Investiture Controversy

159, the year in which *The Play about the Antichrist* was composed, proved to be a particularly significant year for Tegernsee Abbey. Since his investiture by Emperor Frederick in 1155, Abbot Rupert of Neuburg-Falkenstein (r. 1155–1186) had worked to secure greater authority over the abbey's daughter cloister of St. Martin at Dietramszell: a community of Augustinian canons founded in the early twelfth century by an abbot from Tegernsee.[57] Rupert sought to exert what he saw as his rightful authority over the land and its resources—the *vacans possessio* or "unoccupied property" of Dietramszell—by insisting in a letter that their newly-elected canon superior "go to the abbot of the [Tegernsee] monastery in order that he might receive investiture of temporal things by [the abbot] and let him show forth all reverence to the abbot."[58] Rupert also sought support from Albert I of Harthausen, who had been installed as the new Bishop of Freising, Tegernsee's diocese, the previous year. As a further indication of the claim's auspicious timing, Emperor Frederick had appointed a new administrator (*vogt*) for the monastery, Count Berthold III of the loyal Andechs family, to oversee matters of imperial concern. Both Bishop Albert and Count Berthold sided with Tegernsee and Rupert's claim over Dietramszell, which was finally resolved in 1159.[59]

In that final year of the decade, similar tensions also increased between the papacy and the Holy Roman Emperor—the title which Frederick claimed for himself in 1157, in an attempt to negate the pope's traditional role in crowning the "the King of the Romans," a custom inaugurated in 800, when Charlemagne, King of the Franks (r. 768–814), had been given that title.[60] Reignited by the election of Pope Alexander III (r. 1159–1181) in that same year, this next phase of the Investiture Controversy further strained the politics of Europe because Frederick had openly opposed his candidacy. Much of Frederick's resistance, like his new title, stemmed from a disagreement that had occurred at the Diet of Bensançon in 1157, when Alexander (then Cardinal Orlando Bandinelli) had seemed to suggest that the Emperor ruled his territory only as a papal *beneficium* or benefice (that is, with

---

57 For more information on the history of Dietramszell Abbey, see *Die Bistümer der Kirchenprovinz Salzburg*.
58 Rupert of Neuburg-Falkenstein in *Die Tegernseer Briefsammlung* (The Tegernsee Letter Collection), MGH Briefe d. dt. Kaiserzeit, vol. 7, letter 211, 240–41.
59 On the resolution of this matter and Abbot Rupert's account of the court proceedings, see letter 18 from *Die Tegernseer Briefsammlung*, 27–28.
60 On the roots of the Investiture Controversy, its medieval documentation, and modern historiographical narratives, see Blumenthal, *The Investiture Controversy*.

papal favor) and was thus eternally subject to the Bishop of Rome, then Hadrian IV (r. 1154–1159).[61] Furthermore, Alexander took significant interest in reforming the Church so as to take greater control over the affairs of diocesan and monastic communities and their leaders: again challenging secular authorities' involvement in matters that he viewed as solely within the purview of Rome.[62] This unfolding political drama, then, was the immediate public backdrop against which *The Play about the Antichrist* was composed and staged at Tegernsee.

Since the late tenth century, Tegernsee had enjoyed significant political and ecclesiastical autonomy as an imperial abbey; it had been re-founded by Emperor Otto II (r. 973–983), who had granted the monks the free election of their own abbot and exemption from all other duties except those owed to the imperial court. It was also free from the suzerainty of the Bavarian dukes.[63] This historical relationship, and the loyalty it inspired, was further reinforced when Alexander III threw his support behind the canons of Dietramszell, against the claims of Tegernsee, the bishop of Freising, and the emperor. Indeed, it is likely that Tegernsee leaned strongly on imperial favor to counter the opposition of Alexander, who had threatened to use his powers of excommunication if certain estates (*allodia* or allods) were not handled following his wishes.[64] The monks' triumph in 1159 was therefore not merely a local triumph over its own daughter house, but a triumph that resonated in a wider world of papal-imperial geopolitics. It is not a stretch to say that these matters, having been largely resolved in 1159, likely necessitated the creation of the play for training young monastics in maintaining advantageous political relationships to enhance the prospects of the monastery.

The play's staunchly pro-imperial, anti-papal stance is mirrored in its treatment of Frederick's imperial counterpart in the drama and the character of Apostolicus: "the Apostolic One," a sneering reference to the papal claim to sole apostolic authority. Although the Emperor and Apostolicus enter together as part of Ecclesia's retinue, with the Emperor at her left and Apostolicus on her right, their character trajectories diverge significantly from that point forward. Apostolicus remains entirely silent throughout his time on stage and is also physically eclipsed by the other rulers who occupy their own thrones: once he takes his place on the throne of

---

61 For a detailed historical account of the political and ecclesiastical relationship between Emperor Frederick and the papal court, see Freed, *Frederick Barbarossa*; on the initial tensions that arose between the emperor and the pope at Besançon: pp. 201–14; and for information on the breakdown in relations between Frederick and Alexander III: pp. 250–57. See also Munz, *Frederick Barbarossa*.
62 See Sommerville, *Pope Alexander III and the Council of Tours*.
63 A record of this declaration can be found in MGH DD O II/O III, 219–20.
64 See *Die Tegernseer Briefsammlung*, MGH Briefe d. dt. Kaiserzeit, letters 19–20 (28–30), 16 (24), 251–52 (280–82).

Ecclesia, he never leaves that spot nor acts in any way to affect the dramatic action of the play. By contrast, the Emperor plays the starring role in the play's first half, his actions following those scripted for him by Adso. Though his role is somewhat diminished in the second half of the play, when he voluntarily gives up his imperial crown and becomes King of the Teutons, he nonetheless proves a formidable foe against Antichrist's forces and is only defeated by the latter's diabolic trickery.

There is no doubt, then, that the play captures and comments on current events. It also proclaims dramatic performance to be the most effective means through which Tegernsee can enact its pro-imperial agenda. In the first half of the play, the Emperor embarks on a campaign to bring the kings and realms of the world under his submission, deploying the rhetoric of crusade and Roman imperial precedent through his (monastic) ambassadors. This effort culminates in his successful defense of Jerusalem against an attack by the—presumably Muslim, certainly non-Christian—King of Babylon, after which the Emperor dedicates his imperial crown to the Temple as an act of Christian sacrifice. This action serves as a symbolic reminder of Frederick's claim that the Holy Roman Emperor, not the pope, has the power to make (and therefore unmake) himself. The parallels to recent historical events are numerous. Following the success of his first Italian campaign (1154–1155), which had resulted in his coronation as emperor, Frederick was regarded as a capable military leader and formidable political force. In 1157, as noted above, he abandoned the older forms of the imperial title he had inherited from his predecessors, notably Charlemagne and Otto I the Great ("Emperor of the Romans" and "King of the Romans"). In doing so, he exerted his claim to imperial privilege on his own "holy" authority in ways that brought him into conflict with the Holy See.

Bishop Otto of Freising had already promoted this image of the emperor as a master of global affairs, military might, international diplomacy, and Roman law in *The Deeds of Frederick* (*Gesta Friderici*)—a work that was continued after his death by his protégé Rahewin.[65] It is no accident that excerpts from this work were bound together with *The Play about the Antichrist* in the sole extant manuscript copied at Tegernsee.[66] The biography also included copies of letters, decrees, and diplomata: not only to bolster this potent image of Frederick's authority, but to demonstrate how he publicly performed that authority through the person of his envoys and ambassadors—just as the Emperor does in *Antichrist*. In the winter of 1158/1159, for example, as he prepared for his second Italian campaign to subdue the rebellious northern cities, Frederick sent his imperial chancellor, Rainald of Dassal, to secure

---

65 Otto of Freising, *Gesta Friderici*; for an English version, see *The Deeds of Frederick*, trans. Mierow.
66 Excerpts from the *Gesta Friderici* are contained in BSb MS Clm 19411, fols. 10–47.

public oaths of fealty from those cities still loyal to him. The formula is recorded in the *Gesta*:

> I swear that from this time forth I shall be faithful to my lord Frederick, the Emperor of the Romans, against all men, as is my lawful duty to my lord and emperor, and I shall aid him to retain the crown of empire and all its prerogatives in Italy. ... I shall not deprive him of his royal rights here or elsewhere. ... Every command of his, given me personally, or in writing, or through his representative rendering justice, I shall faithfully observe.[67]

The Imperial Ambassadors in *The Play about the Antichrist* likewise demand a similar pledge from each king and kingdom in the play. Though the King of the Franks initially resists swearing fealty to the Emperor, he is subsequently defeated in battle and, perhaps as an example to the other royal characters, becomes the first to speak the oath that is then repeated, in turn, by each ensuing king:

> The awesome reign of empire
>   inspires holy dread.
> Its honor and its glory be
>   forever garlanded!
> Your every right to rule
>   we now acknowledge publicly:
> henceforth with all our willingness
>   we'll serve obediently. (p. 89, 18–25)

This formula echoes the language of imperial authority rooted in the historical and legal precedents that were foundational to Frederick's claims. It is noteworthy that, in that same winter of 1158/1159, Frederick was readying his forces at Augsburg, some eighty miles and just a few days' travel northwest from Tegernsee, and that delegations to and from the imperial camp would have crossed the Brenner Pass and passed by Tegernsee. It is more than likely that the abbey would have been a posting station for imperial delegations like that of Rainald of Dassal, as they traveled into Italy.[68]

The oaths of fealty and submission sworn by the regnal characters in *Antichrist* proclaim the Emperor's right to rule by ancient precedent and recent conquest. This is also the claim made by the Emperor himself, each time he sends his ambassadors on a mission.

---

67 Otto of Freising, *Gesta Friderici*, III:xx; *The Deeds of Frederick*, 195.
68 *The Deeds of Frederick*, 201.

> We're told by those who keep the books
>   and write the history
> that all the world was at one time
>   the Romans' treasury.
> The strength of those who built it first
>   was awesome to behold;
> but then it went from bad to worse
>   when weak men took control.
> Empire, bowed to travesty
>   through men inferior,
> we now with potent majesty
>   will once again restore! (p. 83, 14–25)

This language implies that the "weak" and "inferior" men who had reduced imperial power to "travesty" were those who had been content to see its power eroded by the papacy. The Emperor's actions, by extension, publicly perform the legitimacy of his power over both secular and sacred entities—again, just as Frederick had done in changing his title and publicly demanding fealty to it from the Italian cities.[69] The monks of Tegernsee clearly recognized and borrowed from Emperor Frederick the efficacy of performance in the exertion of power and political will. In that same year, Abbot Rupert described to Bishop Albert the ceremonial reassertion of authority over Dietramszell, stressing that the resolution of the dispute (which had attracted both papal and imperial attention) was affirmed through public and performative means.[70] Thus, *Antichrist* was not a mere *mimetic* representation of medieval publicity but another medium through which Tegernsee publicly bolstered Frederick's imperial authority and the monks' own autonomy as beneficiaries of it. The monks are, after all, "those that keep the books / and write the history."

In a stark contrast, the play relegates Apostolicus, the pope's avatar, to the margins of the drama and deprives him of agency.[71] In doing so, it explicitly reverses

---

69 On the necessity of public and repetitive attestation as a signal of legitimacy in a medieval polity, see Symes, *A Common Stage*, 137–38.
70 Rupert of Neuburg-Falkenstein in *Die Tegernseer Briefsammlung*, MGH Briefe d. dt. Kaiserzeit, letter 211, 241: "Facta hac diffinicione et roborata *publica adtestatione* virorum illustrium et sapientum, qui presentes aderant, de electione eiusdem prepositi ex gratia et benignitate assensum prebuimus et eum ad eandem ecclesiam a vestra benignitate dirigi diligentissime postulamus, si quidem ea, quae superius diffinita sunt, fideliter exequi voluerit." (emphasis added).
71 On this designation as a signifier for the jurisdictional interpretation of Petrine authority embodied by the pope, see Wilks, "*Apostolicus* and the Bishop of Rome," 314–18. Wilks points to the formula "Dominus sanctus et apostolica sede dignissimus episcopus" in the early medieval sources of Marculf, Venantius Fortunatus, Alcuin, etc. Moreover, the documentary appearance and under-

centuries of papal claims to power based on the office's association with Peter, "the rock" (*petros*) of Jesus's apostles. During the early decades of escalating tensions between the German emperors and the papacy, Pope Gregory VII (r. 1073–1085) had invoked his jurisdictional powers as *successor apostolorum* in order to forge a peace treaty with the Norman conquerors of Sicily, claiming that he represented "the Blessed Peter, who [the Normans] desire to have as both leader *and emperor* after God."[72] Gregory's expansion of the traditional authoritative implications of the title *apostolicus* set a precedent that was maintained by succeeding popes. Yet this is belied by the silent, ineffectual Apostolicus who spends the play on the *sedes*, a raised dais or platform, on which the throne of Ecclesia is located. Unlike any other character, Apostolicus never leaves his assigned station. Throughout the proclamations, battles, and apocalyptic events of the play, this figure of papal authority is visibly present to the audience but remains an disengaged spectator of the contestations among political, sacerdotal, and eschatological characters.

This mimetic construction is a foil to that of the skillful, commanding Emperor. Indeed, this dramatic tactic reveals *The Play about the Antichrist* to be a document attesting to "the broader sense of what made law and law-giving authoritative" during the Investiture Controversy.[73] The play mirrors, but reverses, much of the propaganda that had emanated from the papal chanceries and allies of Gregory VII during the height of tensions with Emperor Henry IV, in the latter part of the eleventh century.[74] It asserts that the emperor embodies divine authority—not the pope. Moreover, the adroit playwright builds upon the conventional foundations of that propagandistic discourse to construct an image of the Emperor as the only ordained instrument of divine agency. *The Play about the Antichrist* therefore survives as the most comprehensive and fully realized dramatization of medieval disputation as it emerged from the crucible of the ongoing Investiture Controversy. Through both its scripting and its performance, the play prescribes "a privileged

---

standing of *apostolicus* within monastic contexts begins with the liturgical *Ordo romanus primus* (OR I). For a translation of OR I, see Romano, *Liturgy and Society*, 229–48. Note that Romano's translation of OR I:6 understands *apostolicus* as part of the rubrics for the Pope's daily processionals, indicating when certain actions are to be performed by subordinate bishops and clerics. See also pp. 250–51 for a textual analysis and history of the term *apostolicus* in the context of early medieval *ordines*, as well as its appearance as early as the seventh century in the *Liber Pontificalis*.

72 Gregory VII, *Registrum Gregorii*, MGH Epp. sel. 3.15, 276–77, emphasis added. See also, *Registrum*, I:19, II:40. For more on Gregory's view of Petrine right and succession, see Bisson, *The Crisis of the Twelfth Century*, 88–91; and Wilks, "Apostolicus," 312, n. 8.

73 Cushing, "Law and Disputation," 188–94 at 191.

74 See Melve, *Inventing the Public Sphere*, II:482–83.

space for dramatis personae" that were "integral to legal battle."[75] Though many other contemporary documents contributed to this debate, *Antichrist* creates a space within the cloister at Tegernsee for enacting the imperial agenda.

At the same time, the political and military battleground of the play stages the importance of proper rhetorical training and diplomacy as practiced in the increasingly powerful courts of medieval Europe. The Emperor's ambassadors, speaking on his behalf and embodying the imperial interest, show a masterful command of the *ars dictaminis*—the medieval art of writing letters and prose that, most importantly, taught proper means of address and exchange between authorities. Through their dialogue, they extend the Emperor's own reputation as an effective orator and canny diplomat in medieval global politics.[76] These imperial actors begin their speeches to the other kings and global authorities with a *captatio benevolentiae* or "winning of goodwill," with the goal of cultivating favor with the recipient of the message and opening the dialogue with an amicable tone. By contrast, Antichrist's henchmen, acting in a similar capacity, completely ignore this polite ovation, opting instead to praise the might of Antichrist in what appears to be a strategy of intimidation. The implication is clear. The rhetoric deployed by each group of ambassadors dramatizes two starkly different medieval senses of Aristotelean *ethos*, reflecting the greater intentions behind the actions of both the Emperor and Antichrist. Though each engages in combat with other forces as the plot unfolds, the Emperor's motives and actions are ultimately in the service of a greater eschatological good, while Antichrist is deceptive and overconfident in his interactions, revealing his diabolical nature and aims.

The monastic community at Tegernsee was clearly unafraid to take a strong stance in the longstanding debates surrounding the extent of imperial discretion over matters of ecclesiastical importance. *The Play about the Antichrist* makes a public declaration, using all the media available, that the monks of this cloister support—in the most dramatic terms—the interests of Emperor Frederick. As an imperial abbey or *Reichskloster*, Tegernsee has produced a play in which the pope is depicted as a helpless observer of apocalyptic events, the Antichrist a fiendish and forceful political power broker, and the Emperor an honorable and principled authority. As discussed above, the monastery also had its own motives for main-

---

75 Enders, *Rhetoric and the Origins of Medieval Drama*, 77.
76 The *ars dictaminis* ("art of letter writing" or dictating) was widely taught in the Middle Ages and shaped the format, language, and interaction of medieval courts. Two copies of the most popular instructional texts on the *ars dictaminis*, the *Breviarium de dictamine* by Alberic of Monte Cassino (d. 1088) and the *Praecepta dictaminum* (ca. 1115) by Adalbertus Samaritanus, were bound together with *The Play about the Antichrist* in the surviving manuscript from Tegernsee.

taining imperial favor as a means to exert influence and leverage in legal, political, and ecclesiastical matters. For all of these reasons, Tegernsee (like other imperial abbeys) had long aided in furthering imperial aims and broadcasting imperial propaganda in support of them. The benefits were mutual: for example, Scott Wells has shown how Emperor Henry II (r. 1014–1024) sought to reform the Benedictine *Rule* in an effort to cultivate a "warrior *habitus*" that projected an "image of monasticism as a collective enterprise, at once hierarchical and communal in its structure and demands" through the propagation of documents that "imagined the ideal cloistered life in emphatically bellicose terms."[77] According to Maureen Miller, on whose work Wells builds, narratives of heroic saints, abbots, and priests produced throughout the eleventh century are characterized by language and imagery that specifically gendered the monk as the highest embodiment of masculinity, devoted to a life of manly chastity and playing a leading role in defense of the Church.[78] This representation of monastic masculinity, at once sexually pure and wholly militarized, was strategically crafted to bind imperial monasteries to the imperial cause, strengthening the emperor's control over a network of imperial goods and services administered by these abbeys, a network in which Tegernsee was a central, strategic node within the independent Duchy of Bavaria.

In *Antichrist*, the monks of Tegernsee explicitly connect their monastic self-identity to a militaristic Emperor devoting his service to the divine aims of Christian eschatology. If we recognize that a Tegernsee monk, or perhaps a young postulant in the cloister school, would have played the role of the Emperor/King of the Teutons in any performance, the monastery and its imperial suzerain would be combined and embodied within the monastic warrior *habitus*. The ambassadors of the Emperor and Antichrist, too, participate in the gendered dynamics of diplomacy and warfare as defined by the parameters of imperial propaganda. As Miller points out, clerical masculinity was, in part, defined by a devout protection of the Church "against the depredations of the laity."[79] As the *didascaliae* (stage directions) of the script explain, the Hypocrites in the service of Antichrist not only seek to enact their deceptions upon the laity, they also hide swords under their cloaks which they only reveal when Antichrist is enthroned in Jerusalem. They are explicitly identified with lay lords who have come under the sway of Antichrist and who pledge to place him on the throne. When Antichrist cannot defeat the King of the Teutons (the Emperor) in battle—another sign of the latter's superior mascu-

---

77 Wells, "The Warrior *Habitus*," 57–85 at 57–58.
78 Miller, "Masculinity, Reform, and Clerical Culture," 25–52. See also Wells, "The Warrior *Habitus*," 59, n. 11.
79 Miller, "Masculinity, Reform, and Clerical Culture," 46.

linity—he must resort to deceiving him with false miracles. Throughout all of this, Apostolicus remains silently atop his *sedes*, doing nothing. He can neither protect the laity from further deception nor can he defend Ecclesia, the Church, from the "many insults and beatings" (p. 111, 20) she suffers from the Hypocrites. Apostolicus thereby embodies the "lukewarm" and unmanly impotence that is rebuked in the Biblical Apocalypse of John.[80]

Embodied Education and Mimetic Modeling

An initial reading of *The Play about the Antichrist* today would almost certainly suggest that one of the most challenging dramaturgical features of the play are the many sung speeches that seem to slow the action, especially due to their regular repetition. But to the informed contemporary reader, the playwright displays a deep knowledge of the rhetorical and ritual practices that constituted a shared culture in the European courts (ecclesiastical or princely) in the twelfth century: knowledge that he would have gained at Tegernsee. The speeches therefore provide an opportunity for monastic performers to enact the courtly manners, language, and ceremonial interactions that were vital to successful communication on the stages of European diplomacy. In its manuscript context, the play extends that educational training to future generations of monks. After its initial composition in 1159, the play was copied, some twenty to thirty years later, and then bound together into a codex that also contains epistolary formulae, treatises on rhetoric and letter-writing, excerpts from the biography of Emperor Frederick (the *Gesta Friderici*), and a series of important monastic memoranda known as the Tegernsee Letter Collection. Altogether, these materials were clearly assembled for use within the cloister school. The relationship between the play and its textual neighbors reveals that the monastery had continued to maintain its identity as a center for instruction in the arts of medieval diplomacy and disputation.

The Play about the Antichrist was thus copied into its extant manuscript explicitly to serve the instructional purpose of molding the monastic identity specific to Tegernsee. In preparing the younger monks to operate effectively on the courtly and ecclesiastical stages of Christendom, the monastery itself served as the training ground where performance was an integral part of the community's social, cultural, and ritual life. The *Rule of St. Benedict* (*Regula Benedicti*) had defined the

---

[80] See Revelation 3:16.

monastery as a "school for Lordly servants" (*dominici schola servitii*).[81] Moreover, the work of the monastery, the *opus Dei* or "work of God" was the embodied, performative labor of liturgical song and prayer. As Jan-Dirk Müller asserts, "social learning is transmitted for the most part by means of imitating," through a mimesis that best captures how "courtly behavior adapts itself to visible models."[82] In *The Play about the Antichrist*, Tegernsee distilled that courtly mimesis as integral to the embodied service of the monastic community and its imperial ally.[83]

Nor is this the only instance of Tegernsee's use of drama as a means of instruction. When Emperor Henry IV had instituted his Benedictine reforms in the eleventh century, Tegernsee was already known for the quality of its poetry, its production of liturgical manuscripts, and its expert training of future powerful clerics.[84] Its most famous *magister* (schoolmaster) was the prolific poet Froumund of Tegernsee, who promoted performance as an integral part of monastic education. As *magister*, Froumund inculcated "monastic ideals" through the interactive study of history, law, theology, and a trained proficiency in rhetorical performance.[85] In his surviving letters and poems, he describes how play-acting in the cloister school engaged the minds and attention of the pupils, and he urged his brothers to support and copy his theatrical forms of instruction.[86] Clearly, Froumund understood that learning happens most effectively when the learner embodies a set of practices modeled by the teacher and the community at large.[87] Theatre provided pupils with

---

[81] St. Benedict, *Regula Benedicti, prologus*, 45: "Constituenda est ergo nobis dominici schola servitii," in *La règle de Saint Benoît*, ed. de Vogüé . and Neufville, 1: 422 and 444.

[82] Müller, "Writing – Speech – Image," 35–52 at 37. Müller speaks to visuality as a dominant type of medieval literacy of which performance was a significant medium. For more on a literacy of performance in the Middle Ages, see Enders, "Critical Stages," 317–25.

[83] On the communal practice of instruction in the life of the monastery in the eleventh through the thirteenth centuries, see Long, "High Medieval Monasteries," 42–59.

[84] On the history, identity, and relationships at work at the Tegernsee monastery throughout the twelfth century and how those factors shaped the monastery over the course of the century, see Buttinger, *Das Kloster Tegernsee und sein Beziehungsgefüge im 12. Jahrhundert*.

[85] For more on the wider use of this pedagogy within medieval educational settings extending well into the twelfth century, see Novikoff's chapter, "Scholastic Practices of the Twelfth-Century Renaissance," in *The Medieval Culture of Disputation*, 62–105.

[86] Froumund of Tegernsee, *Codex Epistolarum Tegernseensium (Froumund)*, MGH Epp. Sel. 3. This emphasis on performance as outlined by Froumund is also briefly explored by Carol Symes, "Performance and Preservation," 35–36. The extant manuscript of Froumund's letters, sometimes called the "Ältere Tegernseer Briefsammlung," is housed as BSb Clm 19412. On the edition by Strecker in the MGH, see Schmeidler, "Über die Tegernseer Briefsammlung (Froumund)," 395–429.

[87] The monastic community as a holistically educational journey toward certain ideas and ideals of spiritual Christian practice was influentially posited by Leclercq, *The Love of Learning and the Desire for God*. See also Long, "High Medieval Monasteries," 43–44.

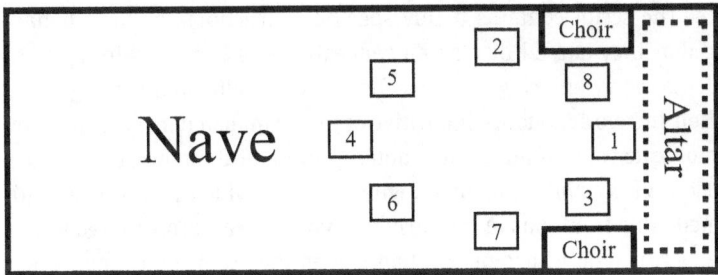

1. Templum Domini
2. Babylon and Gentilitas
3. Synagoga
4. The Emperor
5. King of the Franks
6. King of the Teutons
7. King of the Greeks
8. King of Jerusalem

Figure 4: The positions of the seven *sedes* as imagined for the St. Quirinius Church at Tegernsee Abbey and based upon archeological excavations published in *Die Klosterkirche Tegernsee* by Sixtus Lampl (Credit: Kyle A. Thomas).

a "social framework for monastic learning" that could be translated to the socially-constructed political systems of medieval Europe.[88]

The Play about the Antichrist not only reveals that theatre was important to the everyday lives and pedagogical strategies of the monastery, it also captures the most important aspects of Tegernsee's "brand" that were projected, in actions and rhetoric, beyond the walls of the cloister. This brand is best exemplified by the contrast between the Imperial Ambassadors and Antichrist's Hypocrites. The author or scribe of the play did not see a need to include any stage directions that specifically identify their entrances (though there is mention of the Emperor's men-at-arms) because it would be expected that those ministerial servants would obviously be at his side. In the course of their ambassadorial efforts, they traverse the playing space—likely the abbey's Church of St. Quirinus—as though engaging the global powers of medieval Europe. Thus, the play not only enacts mimesis in its characters but also within space, providing specific directions, where needed, so as to reproduce a world from the signifiers of ambassadorship that were practiced as a part of monastic education. Indeed, the Ambassadors communicate that "distances

---

88 Long, "High Medieval Monasteries," 43.

and space don't exist by themselves ... rather they are created."[89] A good ambassador reduces the distance between his lord and the recipient of a message, bringing them closer in proximity through rhetorical prowess and ministerial service.

By comparison, the Hypocrites enter *before* Antichrist, preparing the way for his appearance. The script contains highly specific instructions for their behavior, explaining that they should display an *"appearance* of humility" in order to manipulate "the laity" by entering "with stealth" and "bending and bowing every which way." Their furtive actions are indicative of the pliant behaviors practiced by certain rival monastic communities: most notably, those of the powerful Burgundian monastery of Cluny and its many daughter-houses, which had broken with traditional Benedictine traditions in the early tenth century and constituted a new monastic order—which, not incidentally, had driven the "reforming" movement launched in the previous century. Their silent, supplicatory, nonverbal regimes of communication may have served as a mimetic model for the Hypocrites. Indeed, not only did Cluny's independence from secular oversight bring the monastery into strong alignment with papal interests, its nonverbal sign-system stood in significant contrast to the practices of monastic oratory and dramaturgy in a community like Tegernsee.[90]

The dramatic function and shape of the characters in the play are also representative of, and work in tandem with, the manuscript as a whole. The play collaborates, as a constituent part of the manuscript, with other texts like *The Deeds of Frederick*, which was one of the most popular—or most utilized—parts of the manuscript (as indicated by the amount of wear);[91] together, they constitute a panegyric in praise of Frederick, the newly established identity of his office as Holy Roman Emperor, and the important role of that office in Christian eschatology. The words, actions, and emotions of the monastic performers imbue within the community a connection to these imperial identities through their role as public deponents of imperial good in the world. Furthermore, the allegorical authority figures represented in many of the characters rely upon the unnamed ambassadors and ministers to carry out their political will and extend their authority into the world of the play. Like these characters and their critical role in unfolding the dramatic action, the accompanying Tegernsee Letter Collection also factors into how the manu-

---

89 Law and Hetherington, "Materialities, Spatialities, and Globalities," 39.
90 On the influence of Cluny, see Bruce, *Silence and Sign Language*, 100–1. The reach of Cluny into the German lands is examined in Cowdrey, *The Cluniacs and the Gregorian Reform*, 191–213. See also Bouchard, "'Feudalism,' Cluny, and the Investiture Controversy," 81–91.
91 Plechl, "Die Tegernseer Handschrift Clm 19411," 445, explains how the pages that contain the *Gesta Friderici* have been worn and yellowed more than the surrounding parchment.

script operates as a documentary collaboration—providing a guide and formula for enacting the specific needs and desires of communities upon the stage of European society. The distinctive theatricality that permeates the manuscript and its function within the monastic setting is further distilled through the theatricality of *The Play about the Antichrist*. The effect of this dramatic compilation is at once wholly educational and also exemplifies a kind of medieval media virality, wherein the embodiment of identity is spread through means of performance—carried not only by manuscripts, but by monks who compose and copy those manuscripts, and who have shaped their own embodied practices according to their theatrical relationship with those manuscripts: one of which demands (p. 101, 1–4) that they "Go and make known" what is happening in the world in order to call for "the help of strong allies who'll soon come to our aid!"

Chapter 3
Liturgies, Æsthetics, and Symbolic Meaning-Making

As indicated in the previous chapter, scholars have long questioned whether there was any specific liturgical setting for the *Ludus de Antichristo*. While E. K. Chambers reached the conclusion that the play fit best within the season of Advent, Karl Young argued that it contained liturgical elements but lacked a distinct occasion for its performance. But what makes a performance or a text "liturgical"—especially given that the term *liturgia* was not commonly in use until many centuries later?[92] Since the works of Chambers and Young, several scholars have responded to the need to interrogate the relationship between a surviving text and what it may convey in regard to dramatic affect and/or performance, especially in the contexts of communal worship.[93] Carol Symes, drawing on the meaning of the original Greek term, describes the liturgy as "the public work of a particular group of people, the shared performances that comes to define that group." Meanwhile, Michael Norton warns "that what we [see] as drama in the liturgy [is] largely a creature of our own making, an imposition of our own understanding of what drama and/or theater might be."[94] Thus, when we speak of "liturgy" here, it is in respect to the communal engagement with familiar performance formats that were commonly practiced in the contexts of monastic settings—whether these formats were utilized in worship, education, social interaction, or other activities.

The history surrounding the creation of this play and the monastic community's intimate familiarity with liturgy as a daily and perpetual performance situate the *Ludus* within both a specific historical epoch and the daily, and seasonal, interactions with the *opus Dei* shaped by repeated rituals and rubrics.[95] Monks spent their lives in the midst of liturgical practice and operated "as embodied repositories of liturgical knowledge gained through oral instruction and memorization over many years."[96] Furthermore, surviving liturgical texts show that there was little consensus among communities regarding the appropriate approach to performing any particular liturgical rite. Individual abbeys like Tegernsee could assert

---

92 See Symes, "Liturgical Texts and Performance Practices."
93 See Norton, *Liturgical Drama*; Petersen, "Liturgical Enactment"; Symes, "Liturgical Texts"; Flanigan, "The Roman Rite"; and Bourgeault, "Liturgical Dramaturgy."
94 Norton, *Liturgical Drama*, 1.
95 A rubric is information that describes or proscribes conditions for the performance of a text; see Symes, "The Medieval Archive," 29–34.
96 Symes, "Liturgical Texts and Performance Practices," 248.

their own interpretive and performative practices or, at the same time, adhere to practices that were common or conventional within specific monastic orders, like the Benedictines.

The Play about the Antichrist is a prime example of how the Tegernsee monks made an organic connection between the theatrical modes of instruction discussed in the previous chapter and performative, liturgical meaning-making.[97] As Symes has explained, the modern definitions of "liturgy" and "liturgical" are anachronisms that have been used to draw misleading generic distinctions among what was really "a wide spectrum of worshipful activities." (The ancient Greek word meant, broadly, the performance of public duties, not merely religious rituals.)[98] Hence, *The Play about the Antichrist* can be described as "liturgical" in that it participates in the ritual work of the monastery and creatively uses a liturgical vocabulary to foreground the monastic actor's central role in the life of the Church—and the wider world. Monks not only perform, uphold, and disseminate liturgical knowledge, they *feel and embody*—on a daily basis—the weight of its mimetic significations. They also take seriously (and playfully) their responsibility to achieve the goals of their community *through* the liturgy. Just as the speeches of the Imperial Ambassadors and Antichrist's Hypocrites dramatize contrasting missions and motives, the association of certain liturgical elements with certain characters and character-groups draws attention to their motivations through an æsthetic that was not only recognizable to a monastic audience, but also largely shared by the highly ritualized elites of both secular and religious spheres.

The affective power of the borrowed liturgical elements embedded in *The Play about the Antichrist* stem from this commonality of experience and what Monique Scheer theorizes as "emotional practice." We can understand their use within the play—and perhaps, its performance in a space associated with the liturgy—as a means to enact the *habitus* of monastic life while also directing the emotional response of the audience.[99] Thus, the play acts as an extension, even interpretation, of Tegernsee's monastic identity by appropriating the community's intimate knowledge of liturgical performance practices and placing them in the service of its pro-imperial courtly agenda, as well its own institutional goals.[100] While there may have been a medieval distinction between (on the one hand) courtly rhetoric and

---

97 Wickham, *The Medieval Theatre*, 29.
98 Symes, "Liturgical Texts and Performance Practices," 239–40.
99 Scheer, "Are Emotions a Kind of Practice," 200 and 205.
100 See Rice, "The Feminine Prehistory of the York *Purification*," 706, on the twelfth- or thirteenth-century effort by the women of St. Leonard's hospital, York, to extend their institutional identity through a Marian play. See also Symes, *A Common Stage*.

the eschatological narrative that drive the play's dialogue and (on the other) the performance of liturgical and ritualized meanings, the dramatic action propelled by the movements and interactions of the play blend the liturgical and the rhetorical to create a truly medieval dramaturgical æsthetic, even as they collapse the distance between apocalypse and the everyday.[101]

This æsthetic was unique, in some ways, to Tegernsee; but it was also a feature of many contemporaneous works that have been variously described as "liturgical" or "dramatic." For example, the *Vos inquam* ("You, I say") was a popular *lectio*, or liturgical reading, taken directly from the fifth-century homily *Contra Judaeos, Paganos et Arianos, sermo de symbolo* (A Sermon on Those Signs that Contradict the Jews, Pagans, and Arians) by the Bishop of Carthage, Quodvultdeus, and later attributed to St. Augustine. This particular sermon was not only widely copied but also gave rise to a popular liturgical trope inspired by its anti-Semitic rhetoric: the *Ordo prophetarum* ("Service of the Prophets") common to several medieval plays.[102] Moreover, the *Ordo prophetarum*'s dramatizations of Old Testament prophesies regarded as foretelling the birth of Jesus as the Messiah made it specifically—if not uniquely—relevant to the Christmas season.[103] *The Play about the Antichrist* accordingly participates in a tradition that treats the liturgy as a shared but malleable discourse and set of symbols that could be recycled and repurposed in new ways.[104]

The liturgical elements chosen for use in this play also mimetically reconstruct the arguments and imagery of the Investiture Controversy, all of which had become widely known even to the laity at large. They specifically target the efforts of the eleventh-century pope Gregory VII to reform and standardize the liturgy based upon "imitation of patristic precedent" (*imitantes antiquos patres*), indicating his

---

101 This idea is expertly articulated by Bourgeault, "Liturgical Dramaturgy," 126–28.
102 See Young, *Ordo Prophetarum*; and Lagueux, "Sermons, Exegesis, and Performance." In what might be considered as the third act of the twelfth-century Anglo-Norman *Ordo representatcionis Ade* ("Play of Adam"), the "Service of the Prophets" opens with a reading of the *Vos inquam*: see the edition and translation of Symes. Likewise, the monastery at Benediktbeuern, only some thirty miles west of Tegernsee, produced the so-called *Play of the Nativity* (*Ludus de Nativitate*), which begins with the *Ordo prophetarum* before moving into the central scene of Christ's nativity. For a recent study, see Drumbl, "Revisiting the Plays of the Codex Buranus."
103 Holdenried, *The Sibyl and Her Scribes*, 82–83; also Fassler, "Sermons, Sacramentaries, and Early Sources for the Office in the Latin West," in *The Divine Office in the Latin Middle Ages*, 15–17 and 21–22.
104 This dramatic treatment of the liturgy in service to the communal engagement is not unique to *The Play about the Antichrist*. On the aims of monastic edification and instruction in the twelfth-century liturgical drama known as the *Danielis ludus* (Play of Daniel) from Benediktbeuern, see Petersen, "*Danielis ludus*: Transforming Clerics in the Twelfth Century."

preference for upholding liturgical rubrics emanating from the Roman rite rather than the many localized and varied traditions.[105] These efforts that were still active in the middle of the twelfth century as "partisan scriptoria" worked to preserve and transmit "the *auctoritas* of Gregory VII."[106] But many communities—especially the venerable Benedictine monasteries that had their own distinctive traditions of innovation and creativity—pushed back against these efforts to impose a top-down, homogeneous liturgical model. As a result, they favored forceful, martial rhetoric in defense of their own practices.[107] As we will see, the liturgical elements in *The Play about the Antichrist* mimetically borrow from the propaganda of Gregorian reform but strategically repurpose it to support Tegernsee's monastic and imperial aims. Although O. B. Hardison has claimed that the appropriation and inclusion of such liturgical material within the dramatic action of a play was *unimportant* to a medieval "theory of drama," it was, in fact, a crucial aspect of medieval stagecraft.[108]

Another crucial aspect of that stagecraft was the arrangement and use of space, which also included the audience. As described in the first chapter, the play opens with detailed, descriptive instructions that emphasize the significance of the playing-space and the meanings ascribed to it in the course of the dramatic action. The first two words of this rubric draw attention to the most primal *sedes*, *Templum domini*, "the Temple of the Lord." Within the later manuscript that contains the play, this mimetic phrase acts as a textual marker that divides the preceding documents from the play itself.[109] In performance, this site also plays a liminal role by situating the performance on the threshold between worldly and divine, present and the future, lived reality and yet-unlived end of days.[110] If the abbey church of

---

105 Gregory VII, *In die resurrectionis*, in *Patrologia Latina*, vol. 148. See Cowdrey, "Pope Gregory VII," 60–61.
106 Robinson, "The Dissemination of the Letters of Pope Gregory VII," 176.
107 The *Micrologus de ecclesiasticis observationibus* (ca. 1085) by Bernhold of Constance defended this Gregorian reform of the liturgy as an "authentic reckoning" (*authenticis rationibus*) while the *Codex Udalrici* (ca. 1125) from Bamberg held that Gregory's letters remained as "weapons of reckoning" in the battle of liturgical reform. The forcefulness of such rhetoric is also a feature of the disputations of Rupert of Deutz (ca. 1075–1129), a Benedictine abbot who not only advocated for traditional monasticism, but who called for monks to take a central and public role in church functions in his *Altercatio monachi et clerici*. See Novikoff, *Medieval Culture of Disputation*, 70–73.
108 Hardison, *Christian Rite and Christian Drama*, 30–33 at 31.
109 On the larger theatrical implications of such textual devices, see Thomas, "The Medieval Space."
110 See Cillers, "Liturgy as a Space for Anticipation," 1–7; and Doig, *Liturgy and Architecture*, especially Chapter 6, "Monasticism, Pilgrimage and the Romanesque," 135–68. See also, Reynolds, "The Liturgy of Clerical Ordination in Early Medieval Art," 27–38.

St. Quirinus at Tegernsee was the initial site of performance, the play conflates that consecrated space with the historical location of the destroyed Second Temple at Jerusalem, which had become the Muslim shrine known as the Dome of the Rock and which, after the First Crusade (1096–1099), had become an Augustinian monastery. Forty years before this play's composition, the *Templum domini* had been the name given to this site by the Knights of the Temple (Knights Templar), a military order founded in 1119. It was therefore a focal point of contested religious heritage, crusading rhetoric, pilgrimage, and transcendent eschatological significance.[111]

The judgment of W. T. H. Jackson that the play provides nothing "to indicate [a] starting point" is thus entirely inaccurate.[112] Practically, the dramatic action begins in the immediate space occupied by the audience in 1159; theologically, it begins at the space occupied by the Jews' Temple of Solomon, twice destroyed and only recently captured by Christians from their Muslim rivals. The church of St. Quirinus is lifted from its everyday monastic moorings and given a powerful centrality, while the audience finds itself on the stage of the medieval world.

Making New Meaning with Repurposed Liturgy

The ensuing examination of the four borrowed liturgical elements in *The Play about the Antichrist* follows the order in which they appear in the script, examining their significance within their new dramatic contexts. To date, no other edition, translation, or analysis of this play has paid any significant attention to these elements, or bothered even to expand their abbreviated rubrics in the manuscript—abbreviated because, for the monks of Tegernsee, they were either well known tropes or texts easily found in the many liturgical books of its library. Of the four, three occur outside the dramatic action that features Antichrist. The one liturgy that includes Antichrist and his Hypocrites, the *Firmetur manus tua* ("Strong is your hand"), dramatically perverts its traditional use as a coronation anthem. The other liturgies retain their performative uses, though not the same meanings or significance as when found in other contemporaneous manuscripts and performances. Shared monastic knowledge of these sung rites is thus foundational to understanding how they would relay meaning in performance. Any deviation would draw attention to the ways in which Antichrist's ascendance is distorting the state of the world and hindering the *opus Dei* of the monastic ministry within it.

---

111 See DiCesare, "The Eschatological Meaning of the *Templum Domini* (the Dome of the Rock) in Jerusalem"; and Kenaan-Kedar, "Symbolic Meaning in Crusader Architecture," 113.
112 Jackson, "Time and Space in the *Ludus de Antichristo*," 2.

Alto consilio

The first such element is signaled by the words *Alto consilio:* an abbreviated *incipit* to a processional liturgy or *conductus* ("song for leading").[113] Although the dramatic action opens with the entrance of Gentilitas and the King of Babylon, the singing of the *Alto consilio divina ratio* ("Through loftiest design, a reckoning divine") signals the entrance of Ecclesia and her retinue (p. 75, 4–9). This liturgy was commonly performed as a part of the Christmas season and alludes to Biblical prophecies of the Nativity and Christ's salvific entrance into the world. Ecclesia, as the embodiment of Christ's Church, is thus brought into the space as proof that Christ's mission on earth has been fulfilled. Her performance of the *conductus* would have cued the audience's sensory recollection of the sounds, sights, smells, and significance of its usual liturgical occasion, enveloping them in the familiar hopefulness of the Christmas season. However, the punctuation of each verse with a metrical refrain sung by her retinue would have sounded a bellicose crusading clarion that constantly disrupted her melody:

> And from this faith all life shall spring!
> O where, O death, is now thy sting?
> If anyone believes contrarily
> We damn him now to Hell eternally! (p. 75, 11–14 et passim)

The serene salvific message of Ecclesia is thus interrupted and challenged. To make a modern analogy, it would be as if a well-loved Victorian Christmas carol was interspersed with the outrage of a punk rock chorus.

In general, a *conductus* was usually sung at the opening processional of a service in which a bishop would enter the church, signaling "the foretelling of Christ's coming through the prophets, and the coming of Christ into the world itself."[114] That a monk performing the role of Ecclesia would take the place of a bishop in this initial ceremonial moment of the play asserts the monastic community's confidence in the centrality of its role in ecclesiastical and eschatological affairs. Furthermore, the song's Messianic language and allusions to the same

---

[113] The earliest extant manuscript containing the *Alto consilio* comes from the abbey at Saint-Martial at Limoges, dated to the late eleventh or early twelfth century: Paris, Bibliothèque nationale de France (BnF) lat. 1139. On that particular *conductus* and its liturgical implications, see Stablein, "Zur Musik des Ludus de Antichristo," 312–27. For information on more widespread versions, including musical settings and notations, see Stevens, *Words and Music in the Middle Ages*, 56–63 and 157–59. See also Handschin, "Conductus-Spicilegien," 104.

[114] Fassler, "The Meaning of Entrance: Liturgical Commentaries and the Introit Tropes," 8–11 at 9.

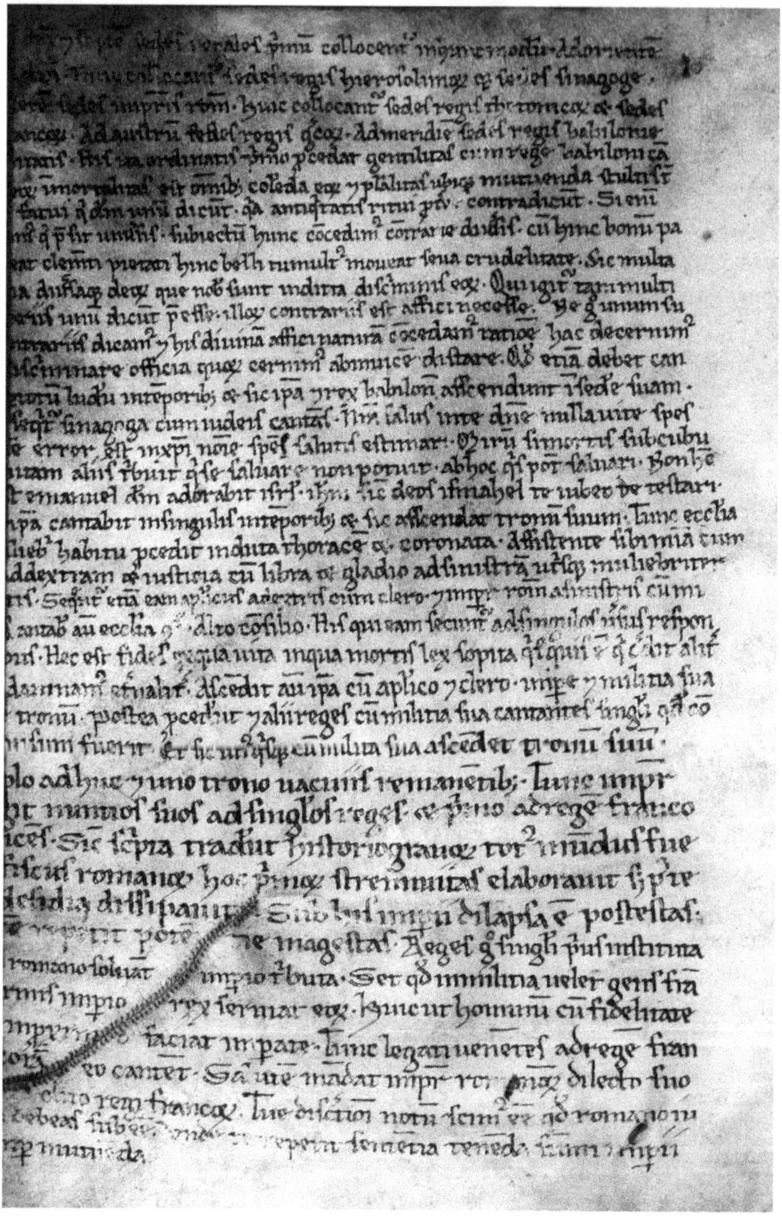

Figure 5: A fragment of *The Play about the Antichrist* contains a copy of the first few scenes, with some minor scribal differences when compared to the Tegernsee manuscript. Notably, though, the scribal notation that indicates the opening of the *Alto consilio* is identical to the Tegernsee edition. From the Abbey of St. Georgenberg in Fiecht (Austria) Stiftsbibliothek MS 234, vol. 4, fol. 39v.

prophetic figures—Moses, Abraham, the Sybil—found in the *Vos inquam* and *Ordo prophetarum* enhances Ecclesia-monk's message by performing the very apocalyptic vigilance for which the contemporary theologian Gerhoh of Reichersberg was appealing in his petitions to the clergy. The inclusion of the *Alto consilio* shines a liturgical spotlight on the monk as the embodiment of the Church. At the same time, the troubling of Ecclesia's triumphant prophecies by the chanting of her Christian followers would be an audible indicator that Ecclesia is also a Church militant and embattled.

Judaea et Jerusalem nolite timere

In response to a call for aid from the King of Jerusalem, the Emperor and his army prepare to do battle with the King of Babylon and so to liberate the besieged Temple of the Lord. Before the Emperor and his forces set out, an Angel appears to bring word of God's assistance, telling them "never should you fear." Then a chorus, with the Angel, sings the liturgical responsory *Judaea et Jerusalem nolite timere* ("Judea and Jerusalem, fear not": p. 103, 23–30). While the chorus of the *Alto consilio* is described as sung simply by "Christians"—members of Ecclesia's retinue, perhaps joined by enthusiastic audience members—it is likely that, following liturgical convention, the play called on the monastery's own choirboys to perform this antiphonal treble chorus.

Like the *Alto consilio*, the *Judaea et Jerusalem nolite timere* is associated with the Christmas season and, specifically, with Christmas Eve. Its inclusion here signals the Emperor's salvific role in the dramatic action of the play, as well as within the political sphere of twelfth-century Christendom (which had come to include the fragile Crusader states of Levant since 1099) and within the eschatological narrative of Latin Christianity. The parallels between these two liturgies connect Ecclesia and the Emperor and show them to be operating jointly with shared Christological aims. And yet, when we consider that the earliest examples of the *Judaea et Jerusalem nolite timere* are extant from no earlier than the beginning of the twelfth century, we recognize that its inclusion in *The Play about the Antichrist* is representative of Tegernsee's cutting-edge connection to other monastic houses and wider European liturgical trends. The earliest known copy of the liturgy appears in an antiphonary from the monastery of Saint-Maur-des-Fossés in what is now a southeastern suburb of Paris.[115] Though there are a couple of extant examples from

---

115 BnF lat.12044.

cathedrals in the twelfth century,[116] most manuscripts were produced in monastic settings. Interestingly, three surviving copies have connections to female communities, including one from the abbey of St. Mechtern near Cologne and another produced at the female side of the dual monastery at Zwiefalten.[117] The specific chants in the antiphonary from that monastery may even have originated at Rupertsberg Abbey, where Hildegard of Bingen served as prioress, before being brought to Zwiefalten.[118]

The connection of this innovative antiphon with female communities suggests that the *Judaea et Jerusalem nolite timere* was included in the play to emphasize the significance of the Virgin as God's chosen vessel, through which the Messiah comes into the world. Its message of divine support for the Emperor and the promise of peace to be restored through his actions is also significant in light of the liturgy's inclusion in a third contemporary manuscript produced for the women's cloister of the dual monastery at Klosterneuburg: the probable source for Tegernsee's version.[119] Klosterneuburg was founded in 1114 by Leopold III of Babenberg in celebration of his wife, Agnes of Waiblingen (ca. 1073–1143) who, through her first marriage to Frederick II, Duke of Swabia (ca. 1050–1105), was grandmother to Emperor Frederick Barbarossa. Any monk or former pupil with a connection to Tegernsee would likely understand the familial allusion and the antiphon's enunciation of Frederick's status as divinely chosen amongst the political elite of medieval Europe. Furthermore, many Bavarian noble families had, since the eleventh century, increasingly turned to the scriptoria of important monasteries to produce documents accounting for their allods and property in the surrounding German lands.[120] Frederick Barbarossa's election as King of Germany in 1152 was seen as an especially savvy political move, due to his familial ties to the two strongest noble houses in southern Germany: the Welfs and the Hohenstaufens. The Welfs had long reigned over the Duchy of Bavaria and Duke Henry XI (r. 1142–1180) was, at the time of the play's initial creation, supportive of Emperor Frederick's efforts to subdue the northern Italian cities. Given the imperial leanings of Tegernsee and its connec-

---

116 Rome, Biblioteca Apostolica Vaticana San Pietro, MS B.79 and Utrecht, Universiteitsbibliotheek, MS 406 (shelfmark 3 J 7).
117 The manuscript from St. Mechtern is archived in Erzbischöfliche Diözesan- und Dombibliothek, MS 1161; the Zwiefalten copy is kept in Karlsruhe at the Badische Landesbibliothek-Musikabteilung, MS Aug. LX.
118 See Hoefener, "From St. Pinnosa to St. Ursula – The Development of the Cult of Cologne's Virgins in Medieval Liturgical Offices," 81–82.
119 Klosterneuburg Augustiner-Chorherrenstift MS Ccl. 1013, fol. 28r.
120 See Freed, "Bavarian Wine and Woolless Sheep: The *Urbar* of Count Sigiboto IV of Falkenstein (1126–ca. 1198)," 71–77; and Noichl, *Codex Falkensteinensis*.

tions to German nobility, it is almost certain that a tacit reference to Agnes in the *Judaea et Jerusalem nolite timere* liturgy was representative of the political good will between the Duchy of Bavaria and the Empire.[121]

Firmetur manus tua et exaltetur dextera tua

The *Firmetur manus tua et exaltetur dextera tua* ("Strong is your hand and high is your right hand": Psalm 89[88]:14b–15) is perhaps the most "exotic" liturgy included in the play because of its apparent origins in early medieval England.[122] Instances of this particular Psalm's use in coronations are found in extant documents that were a part of the pontifical (episcopal) tradition emanating from communities in Winchester, Exeter, and Canterbury by the tenth century.[123] English pontifical manuscripts came to serve as the basis for the Benedictional (prayerbook) associated with Archbishop Robert II of Rouen (r. 989–1037), brother to Emma of Normandy who was the wife of the English King Æthelread II ("the Unrede") and, later, of Cnut the Great of Denmark after his conquest of England.[124] By the end of the eleventh century, the so-called Sherborne Pontifical had also made its way to the Continent, to Notre-Dame of Paris.[125] Furthermore, L. G. Wickham Legg identifies two similar coronation rubrics in later pontifical manuscripts made for the Capetian kings of France and southern Italy.[126] It is important to point out not only the roots of this tradition, but to identify these documents because they hold clues to this Psalm's use in performance that are not found in the surviving manuscript of the play. For

---

121 A similar allusion to a lay individual implicated in the course of liturgical practice can be found in the *Chronicon* of Thietmar of Merseburg (975–1018), when Abbot Liudolf of Corvey, while celebrating the Mass, saw (in a vision) the head of Count Gero of Alsleben. As Thietmar explains, Gero had been sentenced to death by Emperor Otto II on what were perceived by some to be thin if not false charges, straining the relationship between the Emperor, several German lords, and those who believed in his innocence. Abbot Liudolf, according to Thietmar, saw his image on the anniversary date of Count Gero's death and once "he had finished the first mass, he sang a mass for the dead and, after removing his vestments, silently left the church." Thus, Thietmar utilizes the Mass as a common affectual framework within which to insert his own misgivings about the intentions of imperial reform efforts.
122 Legg, *English Coronation Records*, 14. Legg also includes a modern edition, see pp. 15–29.
123 See Richardson, "The Coronation in Medieval England," 136–42.
124 Rouen, Bibliothèque municipale, MS 369 Y.007.
125 Backhouse, *The Sherborne Missal*, 38. On the breadth of the benedictional tradition of the tenth and eleventh centuries, see Conner, *Anglo-Saxon Exeter*, 42–44.
126 Legg, *English Coronation Records*, 14; these manuscripts are the twelfth-century Charles Pontifical, BnF lat. 945 and the fourteenth-century BnF lat. 977.

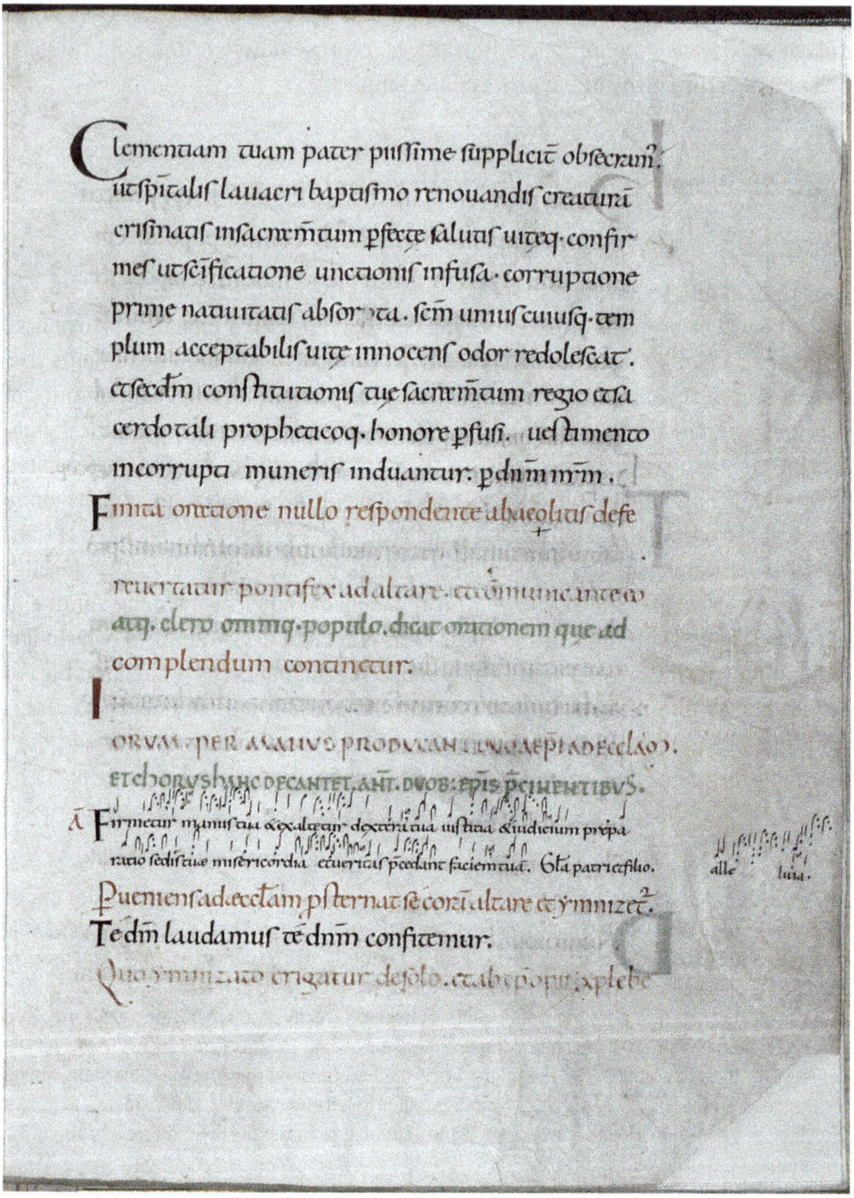
Clementiam tuam pater piissime supplicit obsecram
ut spitalis lauacri baptismo renouandis creaturā
crismatis in sacramentum pfecte salutis uiteq; confir
mes ut scificatione unctionis infusa · corruptione
prime natiuitatis absorpta · scm uniuscuiusq; tem
plum acceptabilis uite innocens odor redolescat.
et secdm constitutionis tue sacramentum regio et sa
cerdotali prophetico q; honore pfusi. uestimento
incorrupti muneris induantur. p dnm nrm.
Finita oratione nullo respondente archiepiscopus defe
reuertatur pontifex ad altare · et comunicante eo
atq; clero omniq; populo. dicat orationem que ad
complendum continetur.
Ā Firmetur manus tua et exaltetur dextera tua iustitia et iudicium prepa
ratio sedis tuae misericordia et ueritas pcedant faciem tuā. Gla patri et filio. alle luia.
Preuenienses ad ecclam p sternat se coram altare et ymnizet.
Te dm laudamus te dnm confitemur.

Figure 6: The incipit, rubric, and musical setting of the *Firmetur manus tua et exaltetur dextera tua* from the Anderson Pontifical, © The British Library Board, BL Add. MS 57337, fol. 57r.

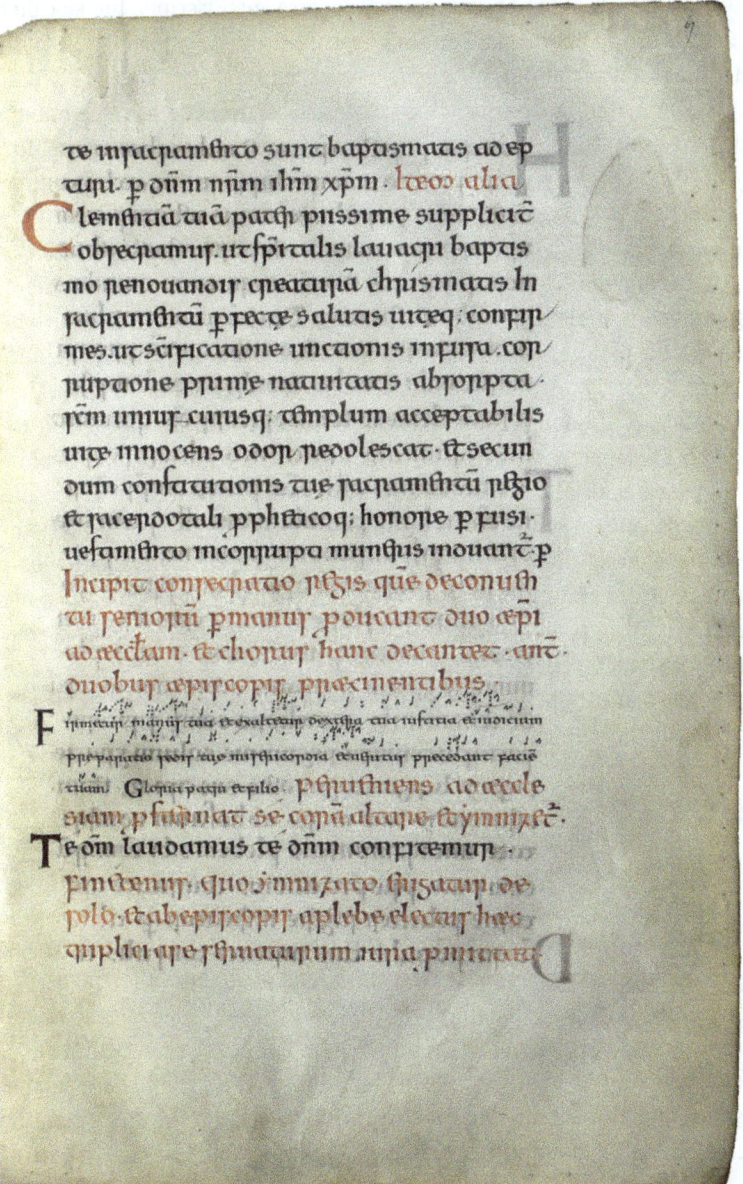

Figure 7: The incipit, rubric, and musical setting of the *Firmetur manus tua et exaltetur dextera tua* from the Sherborne Pontifical, © BnF MS Latin 943, fol. 67r.

example, two of the surviving early medieval English manuscripts, the so-called Anderson Pontifical and Sherborne Pontifical, record the neumatic notation of the plainchant.[127] It is not certain that the music recorded in either pontifical would have been the same used in a performance of *Antichrist*. Nonetheless, the milieus within which the liturgy found significance—royal coronations and pontifical liturgies—were crucial to the work of dramatic meaning-making in the twelfth-century Tegernsee *Ludus de Antichristo*.

The *Firmetur manus tua* operates in much the same mode of performance as the other liturgies included in the play and would surely not have been chosen if the monks—and their audience—were unaware of its associations. Indeed, as with the *Alto consilio*, the play anticipates its familiarity. In the preceding moment, Antichrist speaks to Hypocrisy and affirms his ascension from within the Church, then declares his intent to subdue the nations and "overthrow old laws, proclaim the new" (p. 109, 22). This moment of acclamation proves a sinister analogue to the proscribed royal proclamation found in the pontifical rubrics of earlier manuscripts where, before his consecration by the bishop, the king promises to protect the true peace of the church (*ut ecclesia veram pacem nostro arbitrio in omni tempore servet*), eliminate greed and sinfulness (*ut rapacitates et omnes iniquitates omnibus gradibus interdicam*), and rule with justice and mercy (*ut in omnibus judiciis equitatem et misericordiam precipiam*).

Moreover, the manuscript does not omit performance instructions at this point in the play—as for the *Alto consilio*—but includes directions that prescribe a significant deviation from the traditional performance of the coronation rite. At the moment when Antichrist is crowned on the seat of the King of Jerusalem, the Hypocrites remove their outer garments (*superiora indumenta*), drawing swords that were hidden under their clothing, while singing the *Firmetur manus tua*. The dramatic act of shedding their humble attire to expose the violent proof of their aims reveals, in the words of Maureen Miller, that liturgical garments and their meanings were "not just an effete set of concerns, references, and metaphors. Clerical uses of clothing constituted a language about power that was widely enough understood and compelling enough to contemporaries that it was adopted by competitors."[128]

The view of the world from Tegernsee in the twelfth century would have encompassed seismic shifts in the landscape of socio-political relationships between the lay and ecclesiastical communities of medieval Europe. Since the early part of

---

[127] The Anderson Pontifical: London, British Library Add. MS 57337, fol. 57r; the Sherborne Pontifical: BnF lat. 943, fol. 67r. The other extant document that records the liturgy *sans* neumes is the so-called Samson Pontifical: Cambridge, Corpus Christi College, MS 146 fol. 69v (p. 138).
[128] Miller, *Clothing the Clergy*, 235–36.

the eleventh century, many rulers of central Europe were increasingly reliant on powerful bishops to exert claims of authority over the legal matters and material resources necessary to maintaining stability within their territories. As Angelo Silvestri puts it, by "the end of the first millennium almost all of the towns in northern Italy were led by bishops."[129] For a monastery in the midst of exerting its authority over the Dietramszell cloister of Augustinian canons, while also looking to maintain, if not enhance, its connections to Emperor Frederick, and whose political ambitions seemed boundless, *The Play about the Antichrist* projects concerns about waning monastic influence through the common knowledge of the liturgy. Just as the *Alto consilio* positions the monastic actor as the ideal *habitus* of both ecclesiastical and imperial aims, performatively contrasted with the role of the bishop, the *Firmetur manus tua* takes this critique a step further by re-using a liturgy in which bishops traditionally take a prominent role.

In this case, the deviation in the liturgical performance signals the devious aims of an episcopacy exerting its authority in the service of diabolical ambitions—at least from the perspective of Tegernsee. In the ongoing tensions of the prevailing climate, liturgical ceremonies of political importance (like that of a coronation) affirmed the might of the bishop vis-à-vis lay lordship.[130] Indeed, the regality of the *Firmetur manus tua* was accomplished through the donning of vestments and ceremonial accoutrements, signaling the authority of the celebrant and the solemnity of the rite: "the archbishop [shall] put on full pontificals [... and] the King's ushers and other officers spread the area with carpets and cushions."[131] Thus, the change in the ritual draws attention to the *removal* of vestments and the brandishing of swords by the Hypocrites. It is a moment of high dramatic propaganda that implicates those bishops (and, by extension, their bishoprics) who promote the cause of Antichrist by ignoring, deceiving, or rejecting the laity and lay authority.

Laudem dicite Deo nostro

The final liturgy included in *The Play about the Anitchrist* also makes up the final moment of its performance (p. 151, 24–30). After Antichrist is defeated, the play instructs that Ecclesia sing the *Laudem dicite Deo nostro* ("Give praise to our God": Revelation 19:5), most commonly associated with the celebration of the feast of All Saints (1 November). In fact, the association of this apocalyptic scriptural quotation

---

129 Silvestri, *Power, Politics and Episcopal Authority*, 19.
130 See Bisson, *The Crisis of the Twelfth Century*, 419–21.
131 Legg, *English Coronation Records*, xxvii.

with the All Saints liturgy was widespread across the German-speaking lands of medieval Europe by the twelfth century. Numerous extant breviaries and antiphonals record the musical setting of the liturgy, including manuscripts dated to the twelfth century and earlier from Klosterneuburg and Zwiefalten, among others. Of the liturgies in the play, this is the most ubiquitously documented in contemporaneous manuscripts from across medieval Europe, again emphasizing common knowledge and practices that are fundamental to understanding how the play constructs meaning from liturgical performance.

A simple chant yet profound in its significance, the *Laudem dicite Deo nostro* places Ecclesia-monk at the center of the final moment in performance, this time singing an unaltered and uninterrupted anthem that returns the audience to the dramaturgical starting-point of the play before Antichrist's appearance—adroitly signaled in the preceding instruction that "all return to the faith" (p. 151, 22). As an antiphon also commonly reserved for the daily office of Vespers, observed at sunset, the closing of the play radiates an atmosphere of divine fulfillment and re-establishes the monk as the embodiment of ecclesiastic eminence.[132] Moreover, in this closing moment of the play, the choice of a simple, well-known and *unrhymed* antiphon familiar from the everyday activities of cloistered life conveys an understated beauty and comforting simplicity that uplifts the mundane and celebrates adherence to the ideals of monasticism. It is clear from the instruction "Eccesia begins" that the audience was intended and invited to join in, completing the performance and enclosing it within the intimate communal traditions of the *opus Dei*. It is a final encouraging gesture to any monastic audience from fellow *fratres* at the abbey of Tegernsee.

---

[132] On the material significance of collected saints' imagery, see Holladay, "The Competition for Saints in Medieval Zurich," 41–59.

Part II: **A New Translation and Edition**

Introduction

This new verse translation captures the poetics of the original Latin text by replicating, as faithfully as possible in English, its meters and rhyme schemes. Previous translations have neglected both, or have attempted to keep some versification to the detriment of the text's meaning.[133] Furthermore, no other edition or translation presents the play in full: all maintain the abbreviations of repeated dialogue, while also omitting texts for the crucial liturgical elements of the play discussed in Part I.

Both the translation and the accompanying Latin edition are based on the sole complete extant manuscript, which occupies nearly five folios in Munich, Bayerische Staatsbibliothek, Clm 19411, fols. 2ra–7vb. In the manuscript, the verse drama is unrubricated and presented in *scriptio continua*: lines laid out like prose, with unusually extensive *didascaliae* (instructions or stage directions) which are here indicated in italics. A later hand has attempted to underline these prose passages,[134] but the effort was inconsistent and, in many instances, missed crucial information necessary for performance. Additionally, the medieval scribe(s) who copied the play heavily abbreviated and condensed most of the text, as well as sections of repeated dialogue, in order to save space. Here, we have silently expanded all abbreviated words while supplying the indicated dialogue in square brackets. We have also expanded the *incipits* of the borrowed liturgical chants inserted at key points in the drama, based on contemporaneous sources containing the full texts, and have placed those texts in boldface type. We have otherwise made no changes to the original orthography and punctuation, but have laid out the Latin verse lines so that their changing meters and rhyme schemes are visible.

Meter, Versification, Repetition, and Improvisation

Much of the Latin dialogue, originally either sung or chanted, falls into rhyming couplets of 6 + 7, set in catalectic dactylic tetrameter, with the final catalexis of each line often operating as a *brevis in longa*. The effect is a light, flowing cadence, culminating in a slight *ritardando* at the end of each couplet, signaling deliberation and authority. The play also makes use of iambic metrical feet in 8 + 7 and 8 + 6 con-

---

[133] Hulme's translation, in "Antichrist and Adam" (1925), is the stronger, but it does not keep pace with the meter or rhyme schemes. Wright's *The Play of Antichrist* (1967) follows the meter and rhyme of Gentilitas's entrance song, but then abandons any thoroughgoing observance of either convention. It also features several rather serious errors in translation: see below.

[134] See Plechl, "Die Tegernseer Handschrift Clm 19411," 459.

structions. The final foot of these lines is often trisyllabic, punctuating the rhythm and conveying a sense of closure.

Despite some inconsistencies, this structure was meant to aid in the memorization of the play; it also propels the dramatic action forward with buoyancy and speed. Moments of special dramatic significance are marked by metrical variants that slow the tempo and create an effect of gravitas or foreboding. The sturdy simplicity of the dialogue is also playful, even leaving room for improvisation: the text directs that Synagoga and Gentilitas should each repeat their initial songs "from time to time throughout the whole play" (*per totum ludum in temporibus*: pp. 72–73, 13), which gives those actors license to decide when to interrupt the action. Given that their characters are initially presented as enemies of Christendom, those repetitions might have been intentionally disruptive.

The play also leaves room for changes in taste and emphasis. The *didascalia* describing the procession of kings and their men-at-arms who follow the entrance of Ecclesia, the Emperor, and their retinue merely directs each ruler and his entourage to sing "whatever seems appropriate." This indicates that certain melodies, musical styles, or vernaculars associated with different ethnic groups (perceived or imagined) might be chosen as stereotypical. And we have evidence that there were such stereotypes; for instance, the highly influential theologian Gerhoh of Reichersberg (1093–1169)—a direct contemporary of the play—boasted that his native German "is most readily adapted to singing" compared to other vernaculars, especially Frankish.[135] Remarking on the two nations' typical celebratory responses (when describing the crusaders' victory at Ascalon, in 1099), he observed that "the Teutons were singing as usual, while the Frankish folk were shouting as usual."[136] One of the oldest German songs in existence could date either from this First or the subsequent Second Crusade (1147–1150).

In God's name are we wayfaring	*In gotes namen fara wir,*
And in his grace we're traveling.	*seyner genaden gara wir,*
Now God's might help us all today	*Nu heff uns die gotes kraft*
And his holy grave,	*und das helig grab,*
Where God himself was laid.	*da got selber ynne lag.*
Kyrie eleison	*Kyrieleis*[137]

---

135 Gerhoh, *Commentarius in Psalmos*, 431 (on Psalm 40[39]:3[4]): "maxime in Teutonicis, quorum lingua magis apta est concinnis canticis."
136 Gerhoh, *Commenatrius in Psalmos*, 437: "In quo Teutonici more suo cantates et Fancigene more suo clamantes." On vernacular songs as media for the spread of news and propaganda, see Morris, "Propaganda for War," 93.
137 Müller, ed., *Kreuzzugsdichtung*, 9 (No. 8). Here and below, all English translations are by Symes.

A song such as this would have been a very "appropriate" choice for the King of the Teutons' army.

Rhyme

The playwright(s) of the *Ludus de Antichristo*, in addition to the many other dramatic and æsthetic feats they achieved, were precocious in their commitment to maintaining a pattern of rhymed quatrains for verses in dactylic tetrameter, with couplets or clusters of rhymed triplets for iambic verses. This is another significant mark of Tegernsee's continued artistic vitality and innovation, since the rhyming of Latin verse was a very new stylistic choice in the twelfth century. It was a practice directly influenced (on the one hand) by vernacular poetics, because songs in many vernaculars were being written down for the first time; and (on the other) by Arabic verse-forms, almost always indebted to rhyme, with which Latin Christians would become increasingly familiar in the wake of the Crusades and through the hybrid song cultures of the medieval world.

In fact, rhymed Latin would have been associated, from its beginnings, with crusading songs like the ones that may have informed much of the play's militant musicality. The oldest such song to have been set down in writing, immediately after the First Crusade, was preserved at the abbey of Saint-Martial in Limoges, where it is included in the same manuscript containing the oldest version of the *Alto consilio* conductus featured in the play, as well as the oldest Occitan "liturgical drama," the so-called *Sponsus*.[138]

Jerusalem mirabilis	Jerusalem the marvelous,
urbs beatior aliis,	above all cities beauteous,
quam permanens obtalis,	more everlasting glorious,
gaudentibus te angelis.	angels praise you, wondrous.
Illic debemus pergere	There we'll go with one accord
nostros honores vendere	and sell our lands for this reward:
templum dei adquiere	to win the Temple of the Lord
Sarracenos destruere.	and put the pagans to the sword.[139]

Hence, we discern that the play was tapping into an already-established crusading ethos and poetics.

---

138 See Symes, "The Appearance of Early Vernacular Plays" and "A Few Odd Visits," for discussions of this codex and its vernacular components.
139 Paris, BnF lat. 1139, fol. 50r–v. See Symes, "The Appearance of Early Vernacular Plays" and "A Few Odd Visits."

Antichrist is not only an early extended exercise in rhymed Latin verse, it is probably the oldest extant rhymed Latin drama. The so-called Fleury Playbook (Orléans, Bibliothèque municipale, MS 201 [178], fols. 176–242) contains rhymed Latin plays, but it was compiled in the later twelfth century, possibly (though not certainly) at the royal abbey of Saint-Benoît-sur-Loire. The *Danielis ludus*, also rhymed, dates from after 1230 (London, British Library, MS Egerton 2615, fols. 1r–68v, where it is part of the Office for the Circumcision; incidentally, this is the same manuscript that contains the version of the *Alto consilio* conductus used in the *Ludus de Antichristo*). The partially rhymed Christmas and Passion plays in the Carmina Burana manuscript from Benediktbeuern, copied in the second quarter of the thirteenth century (Munich, Bayerische Staatsbibliothek, Clm 4660/4660a), were almost certainly influenced by *Antichrist* and also feature some rhymed (German) vernacular passages. The only other rhymed Latin play that could be earlier, or contemporary, is the *Suscitio Lazari* (Raising of Lazarus) of Hilarius, self-identified as a pupil of Peter Abelard (1079–1142), which blends rhymed Latin stanzas with those in Anglo-Norman French (Paris, Bibliothèque nationale de France, lat. 11331, fols. 9r–10v).

Didascaliæ (Stage Directions)

The very extensive prose instructions for the staging of the play are another of *Antichrist*'s cutting-edge features, as well as a clear indication that it was meant to circulate widely beyond the purview of the abbey. Most medieval plays and performance traditions were rarely recorded with such care, or in such detail—if at all, especially if they were meant to be used "in house." The "Fleury Playbook," for example, is such a mess that it would hardly be legible to most performers, and its music is so carelessly notated that it would not be singable by anyone not already familiar with the tunes. The earliest extant play in Castilian, the *Auto de los reyes magos* (Play of the Magi Kings), was hastily written out in long lines on the spare leaves at the end of a dog-eared codex, with no character designations, stage directions, or notation of any kind: just a few markings to punctuate changes of singer and scene. It is clearly an aide-mémoire for performers who already knew it well.[140]

Instead, *Ludus de Antichristo* anticipates, and almost certainly provided a model for, the carefully rubricated dramas of nearby Benediktbeuern, which also pay careful attention to setting, stagecraft, and even include instructions to guide

---

140 Symes, "The Appearance of Early Vernacular Plays" and "The Medieval Archive and the History of Theatre." The manuscript is Toledo, Biblioteca de Cabildo, Cax-6, 8, fols. 67v–68r.

particular actors in the performance of their roles. Such ample instructions are also a feature of the Anglo-Norman and Latin *Ordo representacionis Ade* ("Play of Adam"), composed in the later twelfth century and preserved in a sole manuscript from the early thirteenth. This, too, was a play that traveled, and that could even be performed by different communities or troupes of professional actors with varying resources at their disposal.[141]

In any case, this single complete manuscript of the *Ludus de Antichristo* cannot have been the only copy made or in circulation after 1159. This particular copy, modest in appearance and lacking any intitulation (because it would have needed no introduction for this community), was made a generation or so after the play's composition, specifically to be included in a small working codex for use in the abbey's school, bound up with an array of materials for the instruction and edification of Tegernsee monks-in-training or the sons of local elites. Others, more impressive perhaps, would have been sent to the network of Benedictine abbeys in which it was situated: hence the single (heavily abbreviated) page still extant at the remote abbey of St. Georgenberg, now in Austria, which was only about 57 kilometers from Tegernsee. And, of course, the text used to guide the first performance has not survived; unsurprisingly, because it would have received hard usage.

---

[141] Symes, *"Ordo representacionis Ade* (Play of Adam)." The manuscript is Tours, Bibliothèque municipale, 927.

Dramatis Personæ

Gentilitas ~ The female allegorical figure representing the Pagans: that is, Muslims. According to the doctrine of the medieval Roman Church, all pagans must convert to Christianity before the Second Coming of Christ. According to medieval popular belief, as exemplified by this play and other contemporary cultural artefacts such as the *Song of Roland* (written down ca. 1100), Muslims were thought to worship multiple gods.

King of Babylon ~ The Abbasid caliph; at the time of the play, this was the powerful al-Muqtafi (r. 1136–1160). Babylon was a generic term of opprobrium used for any Islamic polity, as well as reference to "the Whore of Babylon" in the Book of Revelation (The Apocalypse).

Synagoga ~ The female allegorical figure representing the Jews; according to the doctrine of the medieval Roman Church, all Jews must convert to Christianity before the Second Coming of Christ.

Ecclesia ~ The female allegorical figure representing the Church.

Mercy and **Justice** ~ Silent female embodiments of these virtues, companions of Ecclesia.

Apostolicus ~ "The Apostolic One," representing the silent and impotent figure of the pope. At the time of the play, this was the newly-elected Alexander III (1159–1181), a nemesis of Frederick Barbarossa.

Emperor ~ This figure represents the Holy Roman Emperor, the title assumed by Frederick Barbarossa in 1157.

Soldiers of Christ ~ Members of Ecclesia's retinue.

Imperial Ambassadors

King of the Franks ~ *Rex Francorum* was the the title borne by French monarchs before the reign of Frederick's younger contemporary and fellow crusader, Philip II "Augustus" (r. 1190–1223), who changed to it to *Rex Franciæ*, "king of France." In 1159, this king was Philip's father, the notoriously pious but ineffectual Louis VII (r. 1137–1180), who was also an ally of Emperor Manuel I Komnenos.

King of the Greeks ~ An insulting and belittling title for the Emperor of Rome, the title borne by the ruler of the eastern Roman Empire with its capital at Constantinople, commonly known today as Byzantium. In 1159, this was Manuel I Komnenos, "the Great," a very capable ruler and general who campaigned against the Seljuq Turks and the Latin Crusader states alike.

King of Jerusalem ~ The Christian ruler of the Crusader state of Jerusalem, established in 1199 and recaptured by the Muslim sultan Ṣalāḥ ad-Dīn (Saladin, r. 1174–1193) in 1189. In 1159, this was Amalric (r. 1136–1174), whose reign saw the rise of Saladin and the effective demise of the kingdom.

Royal Messengers of Jerusalem

Angel and **Chorus**

King of the Teutons ~ The identity assumed by the Emperor after he offers his crown to Ecclesia in the Temple of the Lord. There was no such title in medieval Europe, but *Teutonici* was the preferred term for "Germans" in contemporary Latin texts. Historically, the Teutons were a fierce Germanic tribe that migrated from the Jutland peninsula of Denmark and successfully defeated several Roman legions before being vanquished in the Cimbrian War (105–101 BCE). Those men who survived were sold into slavery as gladiators; the women, rather than submit to being enslaved and raped by their captors, killed their own children and then themselves in a "Teutonic fury," according to Roman historians. In 1192, the Teutonic Order of Knights was founded at Acre, the last outpost of the Christian Crusader kingdom of Jerusalem. A militant quasi-monastic order of German knights, it would launch a new series of crusades against the pagan peoples of Hungary, the Slavic lands, and the Baltic region. It is tempting to think that some of its founding members were among the thousands of German soldiers who arrived in Acre after Frederick's death in Armenia in 1190, on the failed Third Crusade.

Antichrist

Hypocrisy

Hypocrites

Heresy

Ambassadors of Antichrist

A False Cripple

A Fake Leper

Man Pretending to Be Dead

Enoch and **Elijah** ~ Hebrew prophets who, according to Christian tradition, can be identified with the "two witnesses" seen in a vision by John of Patmos (John the Divine) in Revelation 11:1–14.

Ministers of Antichrist

Ludus de Antichristo
edited by Kyle A. Thomas

Templum domini. et VII sedes regales primum collocentur in hunc modum. Ad orientem templum domini. Huic collocantur sedes regis hierosolimorum et sedes sinagogae ad occidentem sedes imperatoris romani. Huic collocantur sedes regis theotoni corum et sedes regis francorum. Ad austrum sedes regis grecorum. Ad meridiem 5
sedes regis babilonie et gentilitatis. His ita ordinatis primo procedat gentilitas cum rege babiloni cantans

[Gentilitas]
    Deorum immortalitas
        est omnibus colenda   10
    eorum et pluralitas
        obique metuenda
    stulti sunt et uera fatui
        qui deum unum dicunt.
    quia antiquitatis ritui   15
        proterue contradicunt.
    Si enim unum credimus
        qui presit uniuersis.
    Subiectum hunc concedimus
        contrarie diuersis.   20
    cum hinc bonum pacis foueat
        clementi pietate
    hinc belli tumultus moueat
        seua crudelitate.
    Sic multa sunt offitia   25
        diuersaque deorum
    que nobis sunt inditia
        discriminis eorum.

The Play about the Antichrist

translated by Carol Symes

The Temple of the Lord[142] and seven royal seats should be set up in this manner at the beginning: in the East, the Temple of the Lord, and grouped around it the seats of the King of Jerusalem and the seat of Synagoga; to the West, the seat of the Roman Emperor and around it the seats of the King of the Teutons and to the Northwest the seat of the King of the Franks; to the South, the seat of the King of the Greeks; to the North, the seat of the King of Babylon and of Gentilitas. When these things are arranged, Gentilitas should come forward first, with the King of Babylon, singing:

[GENTILITAS]
    The gods, undying in their might,
        deserve the praise of all—
    the many gods whom we requite
        with awesome ritual.
    Some idiots and wretched fools
        say god's one deity;
    but following the ancient rules
        we shun such blasphemy.
    If we believed god singular
        in all the universe,
    then we'd believe their actions are
        contrary and diverse:
    that *here* they foster healthful peace
        with gentle clemency
    while *there* destructive wars increase
        through hardened cruelty.
    But see the great variety
        of works the gods perform!
    This proves the separate qualities
        to which each must conform.

---

[142] A setting intended to represent the destroyed Second Temple at Jerusalem, which had become the Muslim shrine known as the Dome of the Rock and which, after the First Crusade (1096–1099), had become an Augustinian monastery. Forty years before this play's composition, the *Templum domini* had been the name given to this site by the Knights of the Temple (Knights Templar), a military order founded in 1119. It was therefore a focal point of contested religious heritage, crusading rhetoric, pilgrimage, and transcendent eschatological significance.

    Qui igitur tam multifariis
      unum dicunt preesse.
    illorum contrariis
      est affici necesse.
    Ne ergo unum subici   5
      contrariis dicamus
    et his divinam affici
      naturam concedamus
    ratione hec decernimus
      deos discriminaret   10
    offitia quorum cernimus
      ab innicem distare.

Quod etiam debet cantare per totum ludum in temporibus et sic ipsa et rex babilonis ascendunt in se dem suam. Tunc seuitur sinagoga cum iudeis cantans

[SYNAGOGA]   15
    Nostra salus in te domine.
    nulla uitae spes in homine
    error est in christi nomine
      spem salutis estimari.
    Mirum si morti subcubuit   20
    qui uitam aliis tribuit.
    qui se saluare non potuit.
      an hoc quis potest saluari.
    Non hunc sed qui est Emmanuel.
    deum ad orabis Israel.   25
    iesum sicut deos ismahel
      te iubeo detestari.

Quod et ipsa cantabit in singulis in temporibus et sic ascendat tronum suum. Tunc ecclesia in muliebri habitu procedit induta thoracem et coronata. assistente sibi misericordia cum oleo ad dextram et iustitia cum libra et gladio ad sinistram utrisque 30
muliebriter indutis. Sequentur etiam eam apostolicus a dextris cum clero. et impera-

>   Thus, they who say a multitude
>   can be contained by one,
>   ascribe to that definitude
>   much contradiction.
> 5   We can't believe there's unity
>   in such a foolish fiction!
>   The nature of divinity
>   admits no such confliction.
>   Our reason prompts us to discern
> 10   that there are separate gods
>   and that their functions, in their turn,
>   are very much at odds.

This [Gentilitas] ought to sing from time to time throughout the whole play. And so she and the King of Babylon ascend to their seat. Then Synagoga follows with the
15 *Jews, singing:*

[SYNAGOGA]
>   Lord, you alone are our salvation.
>   In man no hope of expiation:
>   it's wrong that Christ's name's invocation
> 20   could hope to save the lives of men.
>   How strange that he should happen to be slain
>   who raised the dead and made them live again:
>   no man's salvation can a man ordain
>   who was condemned as he was then.
> 25   This man is not the Lord's Emmanuel,
>   The One to be adored by Israel.
>   This Jesus, like the gods of Ishmael,
>   I bid you curse as he did them.

This Synagoga will also sing from time to time, and so she will ascend to her throne.
30 *Then Ecclesia in womanly attire will come forward, crowned and wearing a breastplate, with Mercy accompanying her (with oil) on her right hand and Justice (with scales and a sword) on her left, both clothed as women. Following after them: Apostolicus, on the right with clergy, and the Roman Emperor, on the left with his men-*

tor romanus a sinistris cum militia. Cantabit autem ecclesia conductus alto consilio. His qui eam secuntur ad singulos uersus respondentibus.

[Ecclesia]

   Alto consilio
   divina ratio   5
     restaurans hominem
   Immitt celitus
   vim sancti spiritus
     qua replete virginem.]

[Milites Christi]   10

  Hec est fides ex qua vita;
  in qua mortis lex sopita.
   quisquis est qui credit aliter.
   hunc dampnamus eternaliter.

[Ecclesia]   15

   Pectus virgineum
     cello capatius
   totum et integrum
     claudit interius
   illum, qui deus est,   20
     et dei filius.]

[Milites Christi]

  Hec est fides ex qua vita;
  in qua mortis lex sopita.
   quisquis est qui credit aliter.   25
   hunc dampnamus eternaliter.]

at-arms. Meanwhile, Ecclesia will sing the conductus "Alto consilio,"[143] to which those [soldiers of Christ] following her should respond after each verse:

[ECCLESIA

Through loftiest design,
5   **a reckoning divine—**
        human faith restoring—
the heavens high send forth
the Holy Spirit's force,
    a Virgin maid fulfilling.]

10 [SOLDIERS OF CHRIST]
    And from this faith all life shall spring!
    O where, O death, is now thy sting?
    If anyone believes contrarily
    We damn him now to Hell eternally!

15 [ECCLESIA

In one breast virginal
    a room was opened wide
where He, healthy and whole
    could close himself inside—
20 **He who is God of all**
    and Son of God beside.]

[SOLDIERS OF CHRIST
    And from this faith all life shall spring!
    O where, O death, is now thy sting?
25   If anyone believes contrarily
    We damn him now to Hell eternally!]

---

143 The text of this *conductus* does not appear in the extant manuscript; the text and notation are supplied in London, British Museum Egerton 2615, fols. 67r–68r, and have been edited by Arlt in *Ein Festoffizium des Mittelalters*, 157–59. This later manuscript was copied between 1227 and 1234 at the cathedral of Beauvais and contains (among other liturgical materials) the Office for the Feast of the Circumcision, otherwise known as the Feast of Fools, within which the *Danielis ludus* (Play of Daniel) is embedded. At Beauvais, the *Alto consilio* was a festive processional anthem (literally, "a song for leading") sung at Second Vespers of that feast. On this and other notated *conductus* in this manuscript, see Ahn, "The Exegetical Function of the Conductus." Alternative notation from other manuscript sources is given by Stäblein, "Zur Musik des Ludus de Antichristo," I: 312–27 at 319–24. See also Stevens, *Words and Music in the Middle Ages*, 59–60.

[Ecclesia
> **Visitatur de sede supera**
> **Babilonis filia misera**
> **persona filii missa non altera**
>> **nostre carnis sumit mortalia.**] 5

[Milites Christi
> Hec est fides ex qua vita;
> in qua mortis lex sopita.
>> quisquis est qui credit aliter.
>> hunc dampnamus eternaliter.] 10

[Ecclesia
> **Moratus est fletus ad vesperum,**
> **matutinum ante luciferum**
> **castitatis egressus uterum**
>> **venit Christus nostra leticia.**] 15

[Milites Christi
> Hec est fides ex qua vita;
> in qua mortis lex sopita.
>> quisquis est qui credit aliter.
>> hunc dampnamus eternaliter.] 20

[Ecclesia
> **Nube carnis maiestatis**
>> **occultans potentiam**
> **pugnaturus non amisit**
>> **armaturam regiam** 25
> **Sed pretendit inimico**
>> **mortalem substantiam.**]

[Milites Christi
> Hec est fides ex qua vita;
> in qua mortis lex sopita. 30
>> quisquis est qui credit aliter.
>> hunc dampnamus eternaliter.]

[ECCLESIA

      Cast down she is from her once lofty throne—
      that wretched whore, daughter of Babylon!
      For now the Spirit sent forth from the Son
5   **lifts up our flesh to immortality!]**

[SOLDIERS OF CHRIST

    And from this faith all life shall spring!
    O where, O death, is now thy sting?
      If anyone believes contrarily
10   We damn him now to Hell eternally!]

[ECCLESIA

    Although the weeping lasts throughout the night
    The morning star heralds coming light:[144]
    From forth the purist womb he takes his flight—
15   **Christ comes, we welcome him most joyfully!]**

[SOLDIERS OF CHRIST

    And from this faith all life shall spring!
    O where, O death, is now thy sting?
      If anyone believes contrarily
20   We damn him now to Hell eternally!]

[ECCLESIA

    In a cloud of flesh the power
      of His majesty He hides.
    Going out to fight He will not
25   **kingly armor set aside!**
    From His enemy He hides the
      mortal essence cloaked inside.][145]

[SOLDIERS OF CHRIST

    And from this faith all life shall spring!
30   O where, O death, is now thy sting?
      If anyone believes contrarily
    We damn him now to Hell eternally!]

---

144   A close paraphrase of Psalm 30:5.
145   These lines prefigure Antichrist's own dissembling of his true nature.

[ECCLESIA
> **Capit deus temporale**
>> **nascendi principium,**
> **sed pudoris non amittit**
>> **virgo privilegium**
> **nec post partum castitatis**
>> **emarcescit lilium.**]

[MILITES CHRISTI
Hec est fides ex qua vita;
in qua mortis lex sopita.
    quisquis est qui credit aliter.
    hunc dampnamus eternaliter.]

[ECCLESIA
> **Rubus ardet, sed ardenti**
> **non nocet vis elementi**
>> **flamma nichil destruit.**
> **Sic virgine pariente,**
> **partu nichil destruente**
>> **virginitas floruit.**]

[MILITES CHRISTI
Hec est fides ex qua vita;
in qua mortis lex sopita.
    quisquis est qui credit aliter.
    hunc dampnamus eternaliter.]

[ECCLESIA
> **Solvitur Abrahe**
>> **sera promissio,**
> **iam fere seculi**
>> **decurso spatio**
> **nobis locutus est**
>> **deus in filio.**]

[MILITES CHRISTI
Hec est fides ex qua vita;

[ECCLESIA

God took on a worldly shape
  the very moment He was born
but by no shame would He allow
  the Virgin's honor to suborn,
nor the whiteness of that Lily
  to be stained with any scorn.]

[SOLDIERS OF CHRIST

And from this faith all life shall spring!
  O where, O death, is now thy sting?
    If anyone believes contrarily
    We damn him now to Hell eternally!]

[ECCLESIA

Burning bush, but in that burning
  its true substance is not turning:
    flames have no efficacy;
so this Virgin, bearing Child,
by this Birth is not defiled:
    flowers everlastingly.][146]

[SOLDIERS OF CHRIST

And from this faith all life shall spring!
  O where, O death, is now thy sting?
    If anyone believes contrarily
    We damn him now to Hell eternally!]

[ECCLESIA

Covenant with Abraham
  soon will be undone,
for the end of time is near,
  now the ages run;
    for to us the Word's made flesh:
    God is in His Son.]

[SOLDIERS OF CHRIST

And from this faith all life shall spring!

---

146 This is a reference to the doctrine of Mary's "perpetual virginity."

              in qua mortis lex sopita.
                     quisquis est qui credit aliter.
                     hunc dampnamus eternaliter.]

[ECCLESIA
              [Cumei carminis   5
                    completur litera:
              Rex, inquid, veniet
                    de sede supera,
              qui presens hominum
                    iudicet opera.]   10

[MILITES CHRISTI
              Hec est fides ex qua vita;
              in qua mortis lex sopita.
                     quisquis est qui credit aliter.
                     hunc dampnamus eternaliter.]   15

[ECCLESIA
              Cum non salvat hominem
                    legis observatio,
              Deus orbem visitat
                    ortu necessario.]   20

[MILITES CHRISTI
              Hec est fides ex qua vita;
              in qua mortis lex sopita.
                     quisquis est qui credit aliter.
                     hunc dampnamus eternaliter.]   25

[ECCLESIA
              Nec per legem gens salvatur
              nec mortuis suscitatur
                    per premissum baculum
              Donec venit Helyseus   30
              et in carne presens deus
                    visitavit speculum.]

O where, O death, is now thy sting?
If anyone believes contrarily
We damn him now to Hell eternally!]

[ECCLESIA

The Sybil's song is now fulfilled,
 as she did prophesy:[147]
the King, she said, is coming down
 from His great throne on high—
who, when He's here, will judge the deeds
 that all men testify.]

[SOLDIERS OF CHRIST

And from this faith all life shall spring!
O where, O death, is now thy sting?
If anyone believes contrarily
We damn him now to Hell eternally!]

[ECCLESIA

For since mankind cannot be saved
 by following the law
God's coming to the world must be
 what He at first foresaw.]

[SOLDIERS OF CHRIST

And from this faith all life shall spring!
O where, O death, is now thy sting?
If anyone believes contrarily
We damn him now to Hell eternally!]

[ECCLESIA

For not by law are people saved,
and not from death are people raised
 by brandishing a rod.
When Elijah comes at last,
in flesh and not in darkened glass,
 he'll see our God.]

---

147 Beginning in the second century CE, some early Christian apologists argued that many prophecies contained in the Roman Syballine Books were references to Jesus Christ.

[MILITES CHRISTI]
  Hec est fides ex qua vita;
  in qua mortis lex sopita.
   quisquis est qui credit aliter.
   hunc dampnamus eternaliter.]   5

Ascendit autem ipsa cum apostolico et clero. imperatore et milita sua eundem tronum. Postea procedunt et alii reges cum militia sua cantantes singuli quod conueniens uisum fuerit. Et sic unus quisqui cum militia sua ascendet tronum suum. Templo adhuc et uno trono uacuis remanen tibus. Tunc imperator dirigit nuntios suos ad singulos. et primo ad regem francorum dicens.   10

[IMPERATOR]
  Sicut scripta tradunt
   historiogravorum
  totus mundus fuerat
   fiscus romanorum.   15
  hoc primorum
   strenuitas elaborauit
  sed posterorum
   desidia dissipauit.
  Sub his imperii   20
   dilapsa est potestas.
  quam nostrae repetit
   potentiae maiestas.
  Reges ergo singuli
   prius instituta   25
  nunc romano soluant
   inperio tributa.
  Sed quod in militia
   ualet gens francorum
  armis imperio   30
   rex servuiat eorum.
  Huic ut hominum

---

13 historiogravorum] Likely *historiographorum* | 27 inperio] Likely *imperio*

[SOLDIERS OF CHRIST
>   And from this faith all life shall spring!
>   O where, O death, is now thy sting?
>   If anyone believes contrarily
>   We damn him now to Hell eternally!]

Ecclesia will then ascend her throne, with Apostolicus and the clergy, while the Emperor and his men-at-arms ascend theirs. Afterward, all the other kings will come forward with their men-at-arms, each singing whatever seems appropriate, and so each one with his men-at-arms will ascend his throne. At this time, the Temple and one throne [that is, that of the King of the Teutons] remains vacant. Then the Emperor sends his messengers to the kings, one by one, first to the King of the Franks, saying:

[EMPEROR]
>   We're told by those who keep the books
>   and write the history
>   that all the world was at one time
>   the Romans' treasury.[148]
>   The strength of those who built it first
>   was awesome to behold;
>   but then it went from bad to worse
>   when weak men took control.
>   Empire, bowed to travesty
>   through men inferior,
>   we now with potent majesty
>   will once again restore!
>   All kings, therefore, who used to pay
>   by former institute,
>   now owe to our new Roman sway
>   imperial tribute.
>   But since in military might
>   the King of Franks is strong,
>   he'll pay by sending men to fight
>   in our imperial throng.
>   To him, then, issue our command—

---

148 Wright translates the word *fiscus* (imperial treasury, "purse") as "fief" (in Latin, *feodum*): an extremely misleading choice which suggests that the play is speaking the language of lordship ("feudalism") rather than that of empire: *The Play of Antichrist*, 45.

>   cum fidelitate
>   nobis in proximo
>   faciat imperate.

Tunc legati uenientes ad regem francorum coram eo cantent.

[LEGATOS IMPERATORIA]   5
>   Salutem mandat   imperator romanorum
>   dilecto suo   inclito regi francorum.
>   Tuae discretioni
>   notum scimus esse
>   quod romano iuri   10
>   tu debeas subesse.
>   Unde te repetit
>   sententia tenenda
>   summi imperii et
>   semper metuenda.   15
>   Cuius ad seruitium
>   nos te inuitamus.
>   et cito uenire
>   sub precepto mandamus.

Quibus ille   20

[REX FRANCORUM]
>   Historiographis si qua fiqes
>   habetur non nos imperio.
>   sed nobis hoc debetur. Illuc enim seniores
>   galli possederunt   25
>   atque suis posteris
>   bonis reliquerunt.
>   Sed hoc inuasori
>   ui nunc spoliamur.
>   absit inuasoribus   30
>   nos obsequamur.

---

22 fiqes] Likely *fides*; though it appears the initial scribe wrote *q* instead of *d*, there was an attempt to correct the mistake by a later hand | **24** A marginal notation (=) that splits the word *seniores* may indicate an elongated line that does not keep with the meter

        him and his men beside.
        Tell him to do what we demand
           and hasten to our side.

Then the ambassadors, coming to the court of the King of the Franks, should sing:

5 [IMPERIAL AMBASSADORS]
        All hail, king, from the Romans' Emperor!
        He greets the King of Franks with great favor!
           Because in all discretion
                we know you to be wise,
10   so now our jurisdiction
                you ought to recognize.
        The law to which, in former times,
                your ancestors adhered
        is still imperial, sublime,
15   and ever to be feared.
        To do his service willingly
                we hereby you invite,
        and to do so speedily
                we eagerly incite.

20 *To which the King of the Franks will say:*

[KING OF THE FRANKS]
        If anything historians say is true,
        imperial power belongs to us, not you!
           For those among our ancestors,
25   the Gauls, to whom it came,
        gave it to their inheritors
                forever to retain.
        So now we're threatened with attack
                upon our sovereignty!
30   We'll beat the brash invaders back!
                We'll never bow the knee!

Tunc legati redeuntes ad imperatorem cantent coram eo.

[LEGATOS IMPERATORIA]
   Ecce franci super te
     nimium elati.
   proterue se opponunt   5
     tuae maiestati.
   Immo et imperii
     tui ius infirmatur
   illud inuasorium
     dum affirmant.   10
   Digna ergo pena
     correpti resipiscant.
   ut per eos alii
     obedire discant.

Tunc imperator cantat.   15

[IMPERATOR]
   Corda solent ante   riuam exaltari.
   superba stultos loqui   nolite mirari.
   Quroum nos superbiam
     certe reprememus.   20
   ac eos subpedibus
     nostris conteremus.
   et qui nunc ut milites
     nolunt ut milites obedire.
   tanquam serui postmodum   25
     coguntur seruire.

Et statim aciebus uadit ad expugnandum regem francorum. qui sibi occurrens congreditur cum eo. et superatus captiuus reducitur ad sedem imperatoris. et sedente imperatore stat coram eo cantans.

[REX FRANCORUM]   30
   Triumphi gloria est   parcere deuictis.
   uictus ego tuis nunc   obsequor edictis.

---

24 The additional repetition of *ut milites* from the previous line appears to be a scribal error

Then the ambassadors, returning to the imperial court, should sing to him:

[IMPERIAL AMBASSADORS]
        Behold! The Franks have made reply,
            but far too haughtily!
5   With crushing words they set themselves
            against your majesty!
        Indeed, they have denied that yours
            is law imperial!
        They call it an invasive force
10   which they will now repel!
        They're worthy therefore to receive
            appropriate redress,
        so others afterward believe
            your word—and acquiesce.

15 *Then the Emperor sings:*

[EMPEROR]
        Hearts leap up high the instant they fall down.
        Don't marvel at the prideful speech of clowns.
           Their overweening pride and their
20   defiance we will meet.
        They'll have to yield to us when they are
            crushed beneath our feet.
        Those knights who now don't wish to fight
            will soon learn to behave:
25   who does not wish to serve as knight
            will have to be a slave.

And immediately, he shall rally his battalions to assault the King of the Franks, who comes out opposing him and who will be led back to the seat of the Emperor as a captive. And when the Emperor is seated, he [the King of the Franks] shall stand
30 *before his [the Emperor's] court, singing:*

[KING OF THE FRANKS]
        To spare the vanquished is the victor's glory:
        So I am vanquished, and yield to your mercy.

          vitam meam simulcum
                regni dignitate.
          positam fateor
                in tua potestate.
          Sed si me pristino   5
                restitues honori.
          erit honor uicti
                laus maxima uictori.

Tunc imperator eum suscipiens in hominem et concedens sibi regnum cantat.

[IMPERATOR]   10
          Viue per gratiam   et suscipe honorem.
          dum me recognoscis   solum imperatorum.

Et ille cum honore dimissus reuer titur in regnum suum cantans.

[REX FRANCORUM]
          Romani nominis   honorem ueneramur.   15
          augusto cesari   seruire gloriamur.
              Cuius imperii
                  uirtus est formidanda.
              honor et gloria
                  maneant ueneranda.   20
              Omnium rectorem
                  te solum profitemur.
              tibi tota mente
                  semper obsequemur.

Tunc imperator dirigens nuntios suos ad regem grecorum cantat.   25

[IMPERATOR]
              Sicut scripta tradunt
                  hystoriographorum
              quicquid habet mundus
                  fiscus est romanorum   30

My life and all that I command—
> divinity of state—
I hereby place into your hand:
> your power is my fate.
5 But if you will restore to me
> the honor I once knew,
The honor to the conquered
> glorifies the victor, too.

Then the Emperor takes him as his man[149] and concedes to him his kingdom, singing:

10 [EMPEROR]
Live in my grace, receive from me honor,
and recognize me as sole emperor.

And the King of the Franks, dismissed with honor, returns to his own kingdom, singing:

15 [KING OF THE FRANKS]
The honor of Rome's name we venerate!
Augustus Cæsar's service makes us great!
> The awesome reign of empire
> > inspires holy dread.
20 Its honor and its glory be
> forever garlanded!
Your every right to rule
> we now acknowledge publicly:
henceforth with all our willingness
25 > we'll serve obediently.

Then the Emperor, sending his messengers to the King of the Greeks, sings:

[EMPEROR]
We're told by those who keep the books
> and write the history
30 that every place on earth once held
> the Romans' treasury.

---

149 A reference to the ceremony of homage, by which a vassal swears fealty to his lord and becomes his man (*homme* in French).

   hoc primorum
     strenuitas elaborauit
   sed posterorum
     desidia dissipauit.
   sub his imperii   5
     dilapsa est potestas.
   quam nostrae repetit
     potentiae maiestas.
   Reges ergo singuli
     prius instituta   10
   nunc romano soluant
     imperio tributa.
   Hoc igitur edictum
     grecis indicate
   et ab ipsis debitum   15
     censum reportate.

Qui uenientes ad regem cantant coram eo. Salutem mandat etc. ibi mutantes

[Legatos Imperatoria
  Salutem mandat   imperator romanorum
  dilecto suo   inclito regi grecorum.   20
    Tuae discretioni
      notum scimus esse
    quod romano iuri
      tu debeas subesse.
    Unde te repetit   25
      sententia tenenda
    summi imperii et
      semper metuenda.]
    Cuius ad seruitium
      te inuitamus.   30
    et tributum dare
      sub precepto mandamus.

Quos ille honeste suscipiens cantat

[Rex Grecorum]
   Romani nominis   honorem ueneramur.   35

       The strength of those who built it first
               was awesome to behold;
       but then it went from bad to worse
               when weak men took control.
5   Empire, bowed to travesty
               through men inferior,
       we now with potent majesty
               will once again restore!
       All kings, therefore, who used to pay
10   by former institute,
       now owe to our new Roman sway
               imperial tribute.
       Therefore this edict vigorous
               to all the Greeks make known
15   and from them carry back to us
               the tribute that they owe.

[The ambassadors], coming to the kingdom [of the Greeks] sing at his court "All hail," etc. with the changes required on this occasion:

       [IMPERIAL AMBASSADORS
20   All hail, king, from the Romans' Emperor!
       He greets the King of Greeks with great favor!
               Because in all discretion
                       we know you to be wise,
               so now our jurisdiction
25   you ought to recognize.
               The law to which, in former times,
                       you ancestors adhered
               is still imperial, sublime,
                       and ever to be feared.]
30   To do his service willingly
               we now do you invite:
       so pay him tribute speedily,
               we eagerly incite.

Receiving them warmly, he sings:

35   [KING OF THE GREEKS]
       The honor of Rome's name we venerate!

tributum cesari   reddere gloriamur. etc.
  [Cuius imperii
      uirtus est formidanda.
  honor et gloria
      maneant ueneranda.
  Omnium rectorem
      te solum profitemur.
  tibi tota mente
      semper obsequemur.]

Eosque cum honore dimittens ipsemet ascendens ad imperium cantans.

[Rex Grecorum]
  Romani nominis etc.   [honorem ueneramur.
  tributum cesari   reddere gloriamur.
    Cuius imperii
        uirtus est formidanda.
    honor et gloria
        maneant ueneranda.
    Omnium rectorem
        te solum profitemur.
    tibi tota mente
        semper obsequemur.]

Qui eum in hominem suscipiens et regnum sibi concedens cantat.

[Imperator]
  Viue per gratiam etc.   [et suscipe honorem.
  dum me recognoscis   solum imperatorum.]

Tunc ille suscepto regno reuertitur cantans.

[Rex Grecorum]
  Romani nominis etc.   [honorem ueneramur.
  tributum cesari   reddere gloriamur.
    Cuius imperii
        uirtus est formidanda.
    honor et gloria
        maneant ueneranda.
    Omnium rectorem

> To pay tribute to Cæsar makes us great!
> > [The awesome reign of empire
> > > inspires holy dread.
> > Its honor and its glory be
> > > forever garlanded!
> > Your every right to rule
> > > we here acknowledge publicly
> > and you with all our willingness
> > > we'll serve obediently.]

Dismissing them with honor, he himself goes up to [the seat of] Empire, singing:

[KING OF THE GREEKS]
> > The honor of Rome's name [we venerate!
> > To pay tribute to Cæsar makes us great!
> > > The awesome reign of empire
> > > > inspires holy dread.
> > > Its honor and its glory be
> > > > forever garlanded!
> > > Your every right to rule
> > > > we here acknowledge publicly
> > > and you with all our willingness
> > > > we'll serve obediently.]

And [the Emperor], taking him as his man and conceding to him his kingdom, sings:

[EMPEROR]
> > Live in my grace, [receive from me honor,
> > > and recognize me as sole emperor.]

Then [the King of the Greeks], having received his kingdom, returns singing:

[KING OF THE GREEKS]
> > The honor of Rome's name [we venerate!
> > To pay tribute to Cæsar makes us great!
> > > The awesome reign of empire
> > > > inspires holy dread.
> > > Its honor and its glory be
> > > > forever garlanded!
> > > Your every right to rule

    te solum profitemur.
  tibi tota mente
    semper obsequemur.]

Tunc iterum dirigit nuntios suos imperator ad regem ierosolimorum dicens.

[IMPERATOR]
  Sicut scripta tradunt etc.
    [hystoriographorum
  quicquid habet mundus
    fiscus est romanorum
  hoc primorum
    strenuitas elaborauit
  sed posterorum
    desidia dissipauit.
  sub his imperii
    dilapsa est potestas.
  quam nostrae repetit
    potentiae maiestas.
  Reges ergo singuli
    prius instituta
  nunc romano soluant
    imperio tributa.
  Hoc igitur edictum
    hierosolym indicate
  et ab ipsis debitum
    censum reportate.]

Qui uenientes ad regem coram eo. c[antent].

[LEGATOS IMPERATORIA]
  Salutem mandat imperator romanorum
  dilecto suo   regi ierosolimorum etc.
    [Tuae discretioni
      notum scimus esse
  quod romano iuri
    tu debeas subesse.
  Unde te repetit

---

23 hierosolym] Supplied, based on the context.

>   we here acknowledge publicly
>   and you with all our willingness
>   we'll serve obediently.]

Then again the Emperor sends his messengers to the King of Jerusalem, saying:

5 [EMPEROR]
>   We're told by those who keep the books
>   [and write the history
>   that every place on earth once held
>   the Romans' treasury.
10   The strength of those who built it first
>   was awesome to behold;
>   but then it went from bad to worse
>   when weak men took control.
>   Empire, bowed to travesty
15   through men inferior,
>   we now with potent majesty
>   will once again restore!
>   All kings, therefore, who used to pay
>   by former institute,
20   now owe to our new Roman sway
>   imperial tribute.
>   Therefore this edict vigorous
>   to Jerusalem make known
>   and from them carry back to us
25   the tribute that they owe.]

[The Ambassadors], coming to the royal court [of Jerusalem] s[ing]:

[IMPERIAL AMBASSADORS]
>   All hail, king, from the Romans' Emperor!
>   He greets Jerusalem with great favor!
30   [Because in all discretion
>   we know you to be wise,
>   so now our jurisdiction
>   you ought to recognize.
>   The law to which, in former times,

>   sententia tenenda
>   summi imperii et
>   semper metuenda.
>   Cuius ad seruitium
>   te inuitamus.   5
>   et tributum dare
>   sub precepto mandamus.]

Quibus ille honeste susceptis cantat.

[Rex Ierosolimis]
>   Romani nominis etc.   [honorem ueneramur.   10
>   tributum cesari   reddere gloriamur.
>   Cuius imperii
>   uirtus est formidanda.
>   honor et gloria
>   maneant ueneranda.   15
>   Omnium rectorem
>   te solum profitemur.
>   tibi tota mente
>   semper obsequemur.]

et ascendens ad imperium cantat. hoc ipsum iterans.   20

[Rex Ierosolimis]
>   Romani nominis etc.   [honorem ueneramur.
>   tributum cesari   reddere gloriamur.
>   Cuius imperii
>   uirtus est formidanda.   25
>   honor et gloria
>   maneant ueneranda.
>   Omnium rectorem
>   te solum profitemur.
>   tibi tota mente   30
>   semper obsequemur.]

Quo ille suscepto concedit sibi regnum.

[Imperator]
>   Viue per gratiam   et suscipe honorem.

              you ancestors adhered
        is still imperial, sublime,
              and ever to be feared.
        To do his service willingly
5   we now do you invite:
        so pay him tribute speedily,
              we eagerly incite.]

Receiving them warmly, he sings:

[KING OF JERUSALEM]
10   The honor of Rome's name [we venerate!
        To pay tribute to Cæsar makes us great!
              The awesome reign of empire
                    inspires holy dread.
              Its honor and its glory be
15   forever garlanded!
              Your every right to rule
                    we here acknowledge publicly
              and you with all our willingness
                    we'll serve obediently.]

20 *And going up to [the seat of] the Empire, he sings, repeating the same thing:*

[KING OF JERUSALEM]
        The honor of Rome's name [we venerate!
        To pay tribute to Cæsar makes us great!
              The awesome reign of empire
25   inspires holy dread.
              Its honor and its glory be
                    forever garlanded!
              Your every right to rule
                    we here acknowledge publicly
30   and you with all our willingness
                    we'll serve obediently.]

For which [the Emperor] receives him and concedes to him his kingdom.

[EMPEROR
        Live in my grace, receive from me honor,

    dum me recognoscis   solum imperatorum.

Tunc ille reuertitur cantans.

Rex Ierosolimis
    Romani nominis   honorem ueneramur.
    tributum cesari   reddere gloriamur.   5
      Cuius imperii
        uirtus est formidanda.
      honor et gloria
        maneant ueneranda.
      Omnium rectorem   10
        te solum profitemur.
      tibi tota mente
        semper obsequemur.]

Ipso itaque reuerso in sedem suam cum iam tota ecclesia subdita sit imperio romano consurgit rex babylonis in medio suorum cantans. 15

[Rex Babylonis]
      Ecce superstitio
        nouitatis uanae
      quam error adinuenit
        sectae christianae.   20
      fere destruxit
        ritum antiquitatis
      et diis subtraxit
        honorem deitatis.
      quorum cultum prorsus   25
        deleri ne sinamus
      nomen christianum
        de terra deleamus
      quod ab eo loco
        debemus inchoare   30
      unde primo cepit
        hec secta pullulare.

Et ordinans acies suas uadit ad obsidendam ierosolimam. Tunc rex ierosolimae dirigit nuntios suos ad imperium cantans.

and recognize me as sole emperor.

Then [the King of Jerusalem] returns, singing:

KING OF JERUSALEM
      The honor of Rome's name we venerate!
5   To pay tribute to Cæsar makes us great!
        The awesome reign of empire
            inspires holy dread.
      Its honor and its glory be
            forever garlanded!
10   Your every right to rule
        we here acknowledge publicly
      and you with all our willingness
        we'll serve obediently.]

And with that, after he returns to his seat, the whole Church will be subject to the
15 *Roman Emperor. Then the King of Babylon will rise up in the midst of his [men], singing:*

[KING OF BABYLON]
      Look at their superstitious rites
        which our true faith insult:
20   the errors now adopted by
        the Christians' silly cult!
      It brings down devastation on
        our ancient obsequies
      and threatens veneration of
25   our honored deities—
      whose worship will be threatened
        if we condone this state!
      The name of Christianity
        we must eradicate!
30   The place where it began to grow
        we ought to occupy—
      that land where this strange sect raised up
        its early infant cry!

And drawing up his battalions, he goes out to besiege Jerusalem. Then the King of
35 *Jerusalem sends messengers to the Empire, singing:*

[Rex Ierosolimis]
>> Ite hec ecclesiae
>>> mala nuntiantes
>> novis auxilium
>>> ab ipsa postulantes.　　　　　　　　　　5
>> Hec dum cognouerit
>>> romanus imperator
>> ispse noster erit
>>> ab hoste liberator

Qui uenientes ad imperium cantant coram eo.　　　10

[Nuntii Regis]
>> Defensor ecclesiae
>>> nostri miserere
>> quos uolunt inimici
>>> domini delere.　　　　　　　　　　15
>> Venerunt gentes in
>>> dei hereditatem.
>> obsidionem tenent.
>>> sanctam ciuitatem.
>> locvm in quo sancti　　　　　　　　　　20
>>> eius pedes steterunt.
>> ritu spurcis simo
>>> contaminare querent.

Quibus ille

[Imperator]　　　　　　　　　　25
>> Ite uestros propere
>>> fratres consolantes.
>> ut nostrum auxilium
>>> laeti postulantes.
>> nos pro certo sciant in　　　　　　　　　　30
>>> proximo uenire.
>> ne ipsis ualeant
>>> hostes superbire.

Qui reuersi stant coram rege cantantes.

[KING OF JERUSALEM]
   Go and make known the vile attack
     that on the Church is made!
   We need the help of strong allies
5   who'll soon come to our aid.
   No doubt the Roman Emperor
     will listen to our pleas:
   He'll be our true deliverer
     from all our enemies.

10 *The messengers, coming to the imperial court, sing to [the Emperor]:*

[ROYAL MESSENGERS]
   Defender of the Holy Church,
     have mercy on our state
   which enemies of God on high
15   seek to annihilate!
   They've come against God's chosen heirs,
     that fearsome multitude!
   The Holy City will be theirs
     if forcibly subdued—
20   the place on which His Holy feet
     once stood and roamed with ease
   they'll speedily contaminate
     with filthy blasphemies.

To them, [the Emperor replies]:

25 [EMPEROR]
   Go quickly back to your own land:
     console your brothers there.
   Our help will ever be at hand
     to those who ask with prayer.
30   Assure them, so they know that we
     move with celerity—
   lest that obnoxious enemy
     achieve ascendancy!

The [messengers], returning, stand before the royal court [of Jerusalem], singing:

[Nuntii Regis]
>Viriliter agens ab
>>hoste sis securus.
>Ad propinquat enim
>>ab hoc redempturus.
>Quem debes in prelio
>>constans prestolari.
>per hunc te gaudebis
>>in breui liberari.

Interim dum imperator colligit exercitum angelus domini subito apparens.

[Angelus]
>Iudea et ierusalem
>>nolite timere
>sciens te auxilium
>>dei cras uidere.
>Nam tui fratres assunt
>>qui te liberabunt
>atque tuos hostes
>>potenter superabunt.

Tunc chorus.

[Angelus et Chorus]
>[R.] **Judea et ierusalem. [nolite timere:**
>>**cras egrediemini, et Dominus erit vobiscum.**
>V. **Constantes estote: videbitis auxilium Domini super vos.**
>>**Cras egrediemini, et Dominus erit vobiscum.**
>R. **Judaea et jerusalem nolite timere:**
>>**cras egrediemini, et Dominus erit vobiscum.**
>V. **Gloria Patri et Filio et Spiritui Sancto:**
>>**Cras egrediemini, et Dominus erit vobiscum.]**

Interim imperator cum suis procedat ad prelium et finito prelio responsorio congrediatur cum rege babylonis. Quo superato et fugam ineunte imperator cum

[ROYAL MESSENGERS]
>With manly courage, fight with faith
>>against this dread regime!
>He's drawing near who's promised us
>>from danger to redeem!
>You ought to press on fearlessly
>>into the bloody fray:
>the more you fight, the more rejoice
>>when he has saved the day!

Meanwhile, as the Emperor musters his army, an Angel of the Lord suddenly appears, singing:

[ANGEL]
>Judea and Jerusalem—
>>never should you fear
>knowing that your help from God
>>tomorrow will appear!
>Your brothers come with firm intent
>>of liberating you,
>While all your potent enemies they'll
>>mightily subdue!

Then a chorus [sings the responsory]:[150]

[ANGEL AND CHORUS]
	[R.]	Judea and Jerusalem, [fear not:
		Go out tomorrow, God will be with you.
	V.	Be steadfast: you will see God's help above.
		Go out tomorrow, God will be with you.
	R.	Judea and Jerusalem, fear not:
		Go out tomorrow, God will be with you.
	V.	Glory to Father, Son, and Holy Ghost:
		Go out tomorrow, God will be with you.]

Meanwhile, the Emperor with his [men-at-arms] goes forth into battle, and when the responsory is finished he joins the King of Babylon in battle. When [the King of Baby-

---

150 This antiphon is usually sung on Christmas Eve. *R* refers to the repeated *responsus* (response), *V* to the *versus*.

suis intret templum. et postquam ibi adorauerit tollens coronam de capite. et tenens eam cum sceptro. et imperio ante altare cantet.

[IMPERATOR]
      Suscipe quod offero
           nam corde benigo   5
      tibi regi regum
           imperium resigno.
      per quem reges regnant.
           qui solus imperator
      dici potes et es   10
           cunctorum gubernator.

Et eis depositis super altare ipse reuertitur in sedem antiqui regni sui. ecclesia que secum descenderat ierosolimam in templo remanente. Tunc cum ecclesia et gentilitas et synagoga iucissim cantant. ut supra. procedant ypocritae sub silentio. et specie humilitatis inclinantes circumquaque et captantes fauorem laicorum ad ultimum omnes conueniant ante ecclesiam et sedem regis ierosolime qui eos honeste suscipiens ex toto se subdet eorum consilio. Statim ingreditur antichristus sub aliis inutus loricam comitan tibus eum ypocrisi a dextris. et heresi a sinistris ad quas ipse cantat.

[ANTICHRISTUS]   20
    Mei regni uenit hora per
    uos ergo sine mora fiat.
        ut conscendam regni solium
        me mundus adoret et non alium.
            Vos adaptas cognoui uos   25
            ad hoc hucusque foui.
        ecce labor uester et industria
        nunc ad hoc sunt mihi necessaria.
            En christum gentes honorant.
            uenerantur et adorant.   30

lon] is overcome and takes flight,[151] *the Emperor with his [troops] enters the Temple. And after having worshipped there, taking the crown from his head and holding it with his scepter and imperial [regalia] before the altar, he should sing:*

[EMPEROR]

        Take what I offer here, my Lord,
            with my most grateful heart.
        I now resign, O King of Kings,
            this my imperial part—
        to You, through whom all kings reign:
            the only Emperor,
        revealing that You ever are
            of all things Governor.

And placing them on the altar he should return to the seat of his ancient kingdom [of the Teutons]. Ecclesia, who went down to Jerusalem with him, shall remain in the Temple. Then, while Ecclesia and Gentilitas and Synagoga sing by turns, as above,[152] *the Hypocrites should come with stealth, bending and bowing every which way with an appearance of humility, trying to gain the good will of the laity. And eventually, all [the Hypocrites] will gather before Ecclesia and the seat of the King of Jerusalem who, receiving them warmly, submits himself entirely to their counsel. Immediately enter Antichrist, wearing under his other clothes a breastplate. And with Hypocrisy accompanying him on his right hand and Heresy on his left, he sings to them:*

[ANTICHRIST]

        My kingdom's hour now has come:
        on earth be sure my will is done.[153]
            My kingship everywhere must be condoned.
            The world must worship me and me alone.
                You're ready for this work, I deem;
                you're cultivated for this scheme.
        Know that your labor and your industry
            to my success are of necessity.
                All peoples venerate Christ's name—
                they worship and adore the same—

---

151 The later action of the play requires the King of Babylon to return to his original throne.
152 After this, the later action of the play requires that Gentilitas retreat to her initial seat, with the King of Babylon.
153 A sinister paraphrase of lines from the Lord's Prayer.

>   eius ergo delete memoriam
>   in me suam transferentes gloriam.
> *Ad ypocrisin.*   In te pono fundamentum.
> *Ad heresim.*   Per te fiet incrementum.
> *Ad ypocrisin.* tu fauorem laicorum exstrue.   5
> *Ad heresim.*   Tu doctrinam clerciorum destrue.

Tunc ille

[Ypocrisis et Heresis]
>   Per nos mundus tibi credet.
>   nomen christi tibi cedet.   10

Ypocrisis.
>   nam per me fauorum dabunt laici.

Heresis.
>   et per me christum negabunt clerici.

Tunc precedent eum ipso paulatim sequente. Et postquam uenerint ente sedem regis 15
ierosolimae. ypocrisis insusurret ypocritis. annuntians eis aduentum antichristi. Qui
statim occurrunt sibi cantantes.

[Ypocritae]
>   Sacra religio
>   iam diu titubauit.   20
>   matrem ecclesiam
>   uanitas occupauit.
>   Vt quid perditio
>   per uiros faleratos.
>   dues non diligit   25
>   seculares prelatos.
>   Ascende culmina
>   regiae potestatis.
>   per te reliquiae
>   mutentur uetustatis.   30

                and now you must erase His memory
                and redirect His glory unto me.
To Hypocrisy: Through you I lay the foundation
To Heresy: on which, with you, I build upon.
To Hypocrisy: You gain the good will of the laity
To Heresy: While you destroy the clerks' theology.

Then [they reply to] him:

[HYPOCRISY AND HERESY]
                Through us, the world will trust in you
                The name of Christ they'll give to you.

HYPOCRISY
                Through me, you'll captivate the laity.

HERESY
                The clergy will deny their Christ through me.

Then they will go forth in front of him, while he follows just a little behind. And when they come before the seat of the King of Jerusalem, Hypocrisy whispers to the Hypocrites, announcing to them the coming of Antichrist. And they shall immediately run to [Antichrist], singing:

[HYPOCRITES]
                Our once-holy religion
                      has long been tottering,
                Our mother Church in vanity
                      has long been languishing.
                Into grave perdition
                      corrupted men will slip;
                Our God would never choose Himself
                      such worldly leadership!
                Ascend, then, to the highest heights
                      of kingly potency!
                All things through you should be made new,
                      by ancient prophecy![154]

---

154 A reference to the Second Coming in Revelation 21:5.

Tunc antichristus.

[A󠀠NTICHRISTUS]
    Quomodo fiet hoc; ego sum uir ignotus.

Tunc ipsi

[Y󠀠POCRITAE] 5
    Nostro consilio mundus fauebit totus.
        Nos occupauimus
            fauorem laicorum
        nunc per te corruat
            doctrina clericorum 10
        Nostris auxiliis
            hunc tronum occupabis
        tu tuis meritis
            certera consummabis.

Tunc antichristus ueniens ante sedem regis ierosolimae cantat ad ypocritas. 15

[A󠀠NTICHRISTUS]
        Quem sub ecclesiae
            gremio concepistis
        longis conatibus
            me tandem genuistis 20
    Ascendem igitur   et regna subiugabo.
    deponam uetera   noua iura dictabo.

Tunc exuentes ei superiora indumenta ascendunt expositis gladiis. et deponentes regem ierosolimis coronant antichristum cantantes.

[Y󠀠POCRITAE] 25
    Firmetur manus tua et exaltetur d[extera] t[ua].
    [justitia et judicium praeparatio sedis tuae

Then Antichrist replies:

[ANTICHRIST]
    How can this be? I am an unknown man.[155]

Then [they reply] to him:

[HYPOCRITES]
    The world is yours—if you go with our plan.
        The public's trust, by our designs,
            has already been won.
    If you corrupt the clergy, then
        the campaign will be done.
    Our help will place you on the throne
        (we know our team's the best).
    Then after that your own talents
        will let you do the rest.

The Antichrist, coming before the seat of the King of Jerusalem, sings to Hypocrisy:

[ANTICHRIST]
    What you conceived within the Church
        in deepest secrecy
    so long ago has now sprung forth:
        you've given birth to me!
    I will ascend the throne, all realms subdue;
    I'll overthrow old things, proclaim the new.[156]

Then throwing off their outer garments, they [that is, the Hypocrites] will go up with drawn swords. And having deposed the King of Jerusalem, they crown Antichrist singing:

[HYPOCRITES]
    Strong is your hand, and high is your right hand:
    [justice and judgment are the habitation of thy throne:

---

155 A crude parody of Mary's words to the angel in the gospel of Luke 1:34, when she hears that she is to become the mother of Jesus: "How can this be since I have not known a man?" (*quomodo fiet istud quoniam virum non cognosco*).
156 A reference to Isaiah 42:9.

misericordia et veritas praecedent faciem tuam.]

Tunc rex ierosolimis ascendit ad regem teotonicorum solus cantans.

[Rex Ierosolimis]
   Deceptus fueram   per speciem bonorum
   ecce destituor   fraude simulatorum.   5
     Regna fastigia
       putabam beata.
     si essent talim
       edictis ordinata.
     Romani culminis   10
       sum eses aduocatus.
     sub honore uiguit
       ecclesiae status.
     Nunc tuae patens est
       malum discessionis.   15
     uiget pestiferae lex
       superstitionis.

Interim ypocrite conducunt antichristum in templum domini ponentes ibi tronum suum. Ecclesia vero que ibi remanserat. multis contumeliis et uerberibus affecta redibit ad sedem apostolici tunc antichristus dirigit nuntios suos ad singulos reges. et 20
primo ad regem grecorum dicens.

[Antichristus]
     Scitis diuinitus
       ab hoc me uobis datum.
     ut per omnes habeam   25
       terras principatum.
     ad hoc idoneos
       ministros uos elegi.

---

24 ab] Likely *ad*

mercy and truth shall go before thy face.]¹⁵⁷

Then the King of Jerusalem goes up to the King of the Teutons alone, singing:

[KING OF JERUSALEM]
    I've been deceived by what seemed to be good!
5   Look, I've been fooled by cunning, skillful hoods!
        The kingdom's blessed summit
            I thought I would attain
    once all these princely edicts
        had duly been ordained.
10   So long as you were guardian
        of Roman dignity,
    the honor of the Holy Church
        grew in security.
    Now, clearly, it was wrong of you
15   to have resigned your post!
    The fatal law of blasphemy
        is growing uppermost.

Meanwhile, the Hypocrites escort Antichrist to the Temple of the Lord, placing him upon his throne. Then Ecclesia (who had remained there) is subjected to many
20 *insults and beatings and will retreat to the seat of Apostolicus. After that, Antichrist will send his ambassadors¹⁵⁸ to the individual kings, and first to the King of the Greeks, saying:*

[ANTICHRIST]
    Know that divinest influence
25   has given this to me:
    that over all the lands I'll have
        supreme authority.
    And to that end, I deem you fit
        to help advance my cause;

---

157 Psalm 89[88]:14b–15; one of the Psalms chanted at Christmas Matins, also used in coronation ceremonies. See Richardson, "The Coronation in Medieval England," 111–202; also Legg, *English Coronation Records*, 86–89. It is likely that the Hypocrites only sing the incipit since the surviving rubrics describe next the donning of vestments, an action that would not fit with the inverted sequence of this ceremony as presented in the script.
158 Later identified as Hypocrisy and the Hypocrites—see below.

>   per quos totus mundus
>   subdatur nostrae legi.
>   Hinc primo terminos
>   grecorum occupate.
>   grecos terroribus   5
>   aut bello subiugate.

Qui uenientes ad regem grecorum cantant coram eo.

[Legati Antichristi]
>   Rex tibi salus sit
>   a saluatore   10
>   nostro regum. et tocius
>   orbis rectore.
>   qui sicut ex scripturis
>   mundo fuit promissus.
>   descendit de celis ab   15
>   arce patris missus.
>   Ille semper idem
>   manens in deitate.
>   ad uitam sua nos
>   inuitat pietate.   20
>   hic se uult a cunctis ut
>   deum uenerari.
>   et a toto mundo se
>   iubet adorari.
>   huius edicti formam   25
>   si tu preteribis.
>   in ore gladii cum
>   tuis interibis.

Quibus ille.

[Rex Grecorum]   30
>   Libenter exhibeo
>   regi famulatum.
>   quem tanto dicitis
>   honore sublimatum.
>   honor est et gloria   35
>   tali obedire

                    through you the whole wide world be
                            made subject to my laws.
                    Hence! seize the kingdom of the Greeks,
                            our first competitor!
5   Subjugate them to my will
                            by terror or by war.

Coming to the King of the Greeks, [the ambassadors] sing to his court:

[AMBASSADORS OF ANTICHRIST]
                    Greetings, king, we bear to you
10   from our esteemed savior,
                    he who redeemed our own kingdom—
                            the whole globe's governor;
                    the one who, as the Scriptures say,
                            was promised to the world,
15   who has descended from on high
                            sent by the Father's word.
                    He evermore remaining there,
                            in all his deity
                    invites us all to life in him
20   through his great piety.
                    He wishes everyone on earth
                            his godhead to proclaim;
                    in fact, he orders all the world
                            to venerate his name.
25   But if with this new edict's terms
                            you don't choose to comply,
                    upon the edge of his sharp sword
                            you should prepare to die.

[The King of the Greeks replies] to them:

30 [KING OF THE GREEKS]
                    I freely do profess my abject
                            service to a king
                    who's so exalted, as you've said—
                            who merits honoring!
35   In fact, it is an honor and
                            a glory to obey.

huic tota mente
desidero seruire.

Et hoc iterans uenit ad presentiam antichristi et stans coram eo cantat.

[Rex Grecorum]
Tibi profiteor 5
decus imperiale.
quo tibi seruiam ius
postulo regale.

Et flexo genu offert ei coronam. Tunc antichristus depingens primam litteram nominis sui. regi et comnibus suis in fronte et coronam ei in capite reponens cantat. 10

[Antichristus]
Viue per gratiam
et suscipe honorem
dum me recognoscis
cunctorum creatorem. 15

Iterum antichristus dirigit ypocritas ad regem francorum cum muneribus dicens.

[Antichristus]
Hec munera regi
francorum offeretis
quem cum suis ad nos per 20
illa conuertetis.
Hi nostro ritui
formam adinuenere.
nostro aduentui
preparauere. 25

>   I want to serve with all my heart
>   and mind in every way.[159]

And repeating this, he comes into the presence of Antichrist and, standing before his court, he sings:

5 [KING OF THE GREEKS]
>   To you I profess publicly
>   your might imperial.
>   I ask that you accept my service
>   to your kingly rule.

10 *And with bended knee, he offers [his] crown to him. Then Antichrist, marking the first letter of his name on the forehead of the king and all his companions, and replacing the crown on his head, sings:*

[ANTICHRIST]
>   Live through my grace and you'll receive
15   the honor that it brings—
>   so long as you acknowledge me
>   creator of all things.

Then [the King of the Greeks] returns to his seat. Again the Antichrist sends Hypocrisy to the King of the Franks, saying:

20 [ANTICHRIST]
>   These gifts are for the King of Franks:
>   they'll help him to decide
>   that he should be, with all his men,
>   converted to our side.
25   The forms of all our rituals
>   they already observe,
>   The pathway for our present course
>   they've helped us to preserve.

---

159 This hasty capitulation, in contrast to that of kings who take greater convincing on the part of the Hypocrites, may be reflective of imperial sentiment toward Eastern Roman Emperor Manuel I Komnenos, who publicly backed the ascension of Alexander III to the Latin Roman Papacy over Emperor Frederick's choice of Victor IV. Animosity is further implied in styling his dramatic avatar as "King of the Greeks" rather than "Emperor of the Romans."

Horum subtilitas
>nobis elaborauit.
tronum consecendere
>quem uirtus occupauit.

Tunc ypcritae acceptis muneribus ai abunt ad regem francorum et stantes coram eo cantant. 5

[Ypocritae]
>Rex tibi salus sit etc.
>>[a saluatore
>nostro regum. et tocius   10
>>orbis rectore.
>qui sicut ex scripturis
>>mundo fuit promissus.
>descendit de celis ab
>>arce patris missus.   15
>Ille semper idem
>>manens in deitate.
>ad uitam sua nos
>>inuitat pietate.
>hic se uult a cunctis ut   20
>>deum uenerari.
>et a toto mundo se
>>iubet adorari.]
>Sed de tui regni
>>certus deuotione.   25
>rependit tibi uicem
>>uoluntatis bonae.

Tunc rex acceptis muneribus cantat.

[Rex Francorum]
>Libenter exhibeo etc.   30
>>[regi famulatum.
>quem tanto dicitis

---

5 abunt] Likely *addunt*; referring to the Hypocrites who have entered the court of the King of the Franks | **23** At this point in the text (and, indeed, in the following speeches) there is the instruction that *utlimam clausulam ista commutantes*

                    Their subtlety and cunning have
                            helped us to occupy
                    the throne which, through our manly strength
                            we now indemnify.[160]

5   *Then the Hypocrites, receiving the gifts, advance to the King of the Franks and, standing at his court, they sing (changing the last clause as follows):*

    [HYPOCRITES]
                    Greetings king! We bear to you
                            [from our esteemed savior
10   he who redeemed our own kingdom—
                            the whole globe's governor;
                    the one who, as the Scriptures say,
                            was promised to the world,
                    who has descended from on high
15   sent by the Father's word.
                    He evermore remaining there,
                            in all deity,
                    invites us all to life in him
                            through his great piety.
20   He wishes everyone on earth
                            his godhead to proclaim;
                    in fact, he orders all the world
                            to venerate his name.]
                    But since your kingdom he is told
25   is sure of loyalty,
                    he sends to you these good-will gifts
                            as proof of clemency.

Then the King, accepting the gifts, sings:

    [KING OF THE FRANKS]
30   I freely do profess [my abject
                            service to a king
                    who's so exalted, as you've said,

---

[160] These lines are jeering references to the French monarchy's support of the papacy and its reforming projects, as well as its opposition to Frederick's imperial claim; they insinuate that these tactics have laid the groundwork for Antichrist.

     honore sublimatum.
    honor est et gloria
      tali obedire
    huic tota mente
       desidero seruire.]   5

Et hoc iterans uenit ad presentiam antichristi. et flexo genu offert ei coronam cantans.

[Rex Francorum]
     Tibi profiteor etc.
      [decus imperiale.
    quo tibi seruiam ius   10
      postulo regale.]

Antichristus eo suscepto in osculum signans eum et suos in frontibus et imponens ei coronam cantat.

[Antichristus]
     Viue per gratiam etc.   15
      [et suscipe honorem
    dum me recognoscis
      cunctorum creatorem.]

Tunc iterum dirigit ypocritas ad regem teotonicorum cantans.

[Antichristus]   20
     Excellens est in armis
       ius teotonicorum
    sicut testantur experti
      robur eorum
    Regem muneribus est   25
     opus mitigari.
    est cum teotonicis
      incautum preliari.
    Hi secum pugnantibus
      sunt pessima pestis.   30
    hos nobis subicite
      donis si potestis.

     who merits honoring!
    In fact, it is an honor and
      a glory to obey.
    I want to serve with all my heart
5   and mind in every way.]

And repeating this, he comes into the presence of Antichrist. And with bended knee he offers him the crown, singing:

[KING OF THE FRANKS]
    To you I profess [publicly
10   your might imperial.
    I ask that you accept my service
      to your kingly rule.]

Antichrist receives him with a kiss, signing him and his [men] on the forehead. And bestowing on him the crown, he sings:

15 [ANTICHRIST]
    Live through my grace [and you'll receive
      the honor that it brings—
    So long as you acknowledge me
      creator of all things.]

20 *Then again the Antichrist sends Hypocrisy to the King of the Teutons, singing:*

[ANTICHRIST]
    Excellence in arms has been
      the Teuton race's law—
    and so the vigor of their skill
25   has testified to all.
    Your task, then: to deploy these gifts
      and make their kingdom yield,
    for it would be incautious to
      provoke them to the field.
30   They who engage them in a fight
      are sure to fare the worst,
    so subjugate them with our gifts
      if you can do that first.

Tunc ypocritae acceptis muneribus transeunt ad gerem cantantes coram eo.

[Ypocritae]
  Rex tibi salus sit. etc.
    [a saluatore
  nostro regum. et tocius   5
    orbis rectore.
  qui sicut ex scripturis
    mundo fuit promissus.
  descendit de celis ab
    arce patris missus.   10
  Ille semper idem
    manens in deitate.
  ad uitam sua nos
    inuitat pietate.
  hic se uult a cunctis ut   15
    deum uenerari.
  et a toto mundo se
    iubet adorari.]
  Et his te honorans
    muneribus absentem   20
  amicum cernere
    desiderat presentem.

Tunc rex teotonicorum cantat.

[Rex Teotonicorum]
  Fraudis uersutias   25
    compellor experiri.
  per quas nequitia uestra
    solet mentiri.
  Sub forma ueritas
    uir tutis putabatur.   30
  ostendit falsitas quod
    forma mentiatur.
  Per uos corrupta est
    fides christianorum
  per me conteretur   35
    regnum simulatorum.

Then the Hypocrites, receiving the gifts, cross over to the King [of the Teutons], singing before his court and again changing the last verse as follows:

[HYPOCRITES]
        Greetings, king, we bear to you
5   [from our esteemed savior
        he who redeemed our own kingdom—
            the whole globe's governor;
        the one who, as the Scriptures say,
            was promised to the world,
10   who has descended from on high
            sent by the Father's word.
        He evermore remaining there,
            in all his deity,
        invites us all to life in him
15   through his great piety.
        He wishes everyone on earth
            his godhead to proclaim;
        in fact, he orders all the world
            to venerate his name.]
20   But you he honors with these gifts:
            to you we him commend,
        who wishes through these offerings
            to show himself your friend.

Then the King of the Teutons sings:

25 [KING OF THE TEUTONS]
        I am compelled to test these tricks
            and show them to be lies
        by which your rank iniquity
            is usually disguised.
30   Beneath such forms of virtue will
            the truth appear revealed,
        but falsity may be the "truth"
            which these forms have concealed.
        Through you the faith of Christians is
35   corrupted and condemned;
        through me the reign of your deceit
            will soon be at an end.

Plena sunt fraudibus
    munera deceptoris.
in quos corruet per
    gladium ultoris.
Secum pecunia sit 5
    in perditionem.
grauem iniuria
    exspectat ultionem.

Tunc ypocritae confusi redeunt et stantes coram antichristo c[antant].

[Y<small>POCRITAE</small>] 10
    O regni gloria
        caput totius mundi
    offensa aspice
        populi furibunda.
    Certe predictem est 15
        per fidem antiquorum
    quod tu subities
        cercuices superborum.
    Si uirtute tua
        totus orbis subsistit. 20
    qua ui teotonicorum
        furor tibi resistit? *Igitur.*
    Tuam germania
        blasphemat dicionem
    extollit cornua 25
        contra religionem.
    respice nostram confusionem.
        in ea iudica tuam offensionem.
    Tuam potentiam
        iniuria testatur. 30
    cuius imperio
        ruinam cominatur.

Tunc antichristus.

---

14 furibunda] Likely *furibundi*. It may be that a later scribe attempted to correct the mistake with what appears to a scratch through the *a* to make it look more like *i*

>   The gifts of a deceiver: these
>   are always full of lies!
>   The sword of an avenger they
>   will disillusionize.
> 5   All these pretentious properties
>   will fall to your reward[161]
>   when you and all your injuries
>   have perished on my sword!

Then the Hypocrites, confounded, return. And standing before the court of Antichrist, they s[ing]:

[HYPOCRITES]
>   O glorious sovereign of the realm
>   and head of all the world,
>   behold the shocking insults that
> 15   these crazy people hurl!
>   It's certainly predicted by
>   the faith of ancient days
>   that you will overcome the proud[162]
>   and bend them to your sway.
> 20   If by your virtue this wide globe
>   is in your vassalage,
>   how can the mighty Teuton race
>   withstand your jealous rage?
>   Look, they blaspheme against your word,
> 25   this rebel German horde!
>   They shake defiant horns against
>   your true religion, lord!
>   Look, we're confused by this offense!
>   Condemn their rash impertinence!
> 30   Let all your power testify
>   against these injuries,
>   which your imperial command
>   will turn to miseries!

Then Antichrist:

---

161 Cf. Acts 8:20.
162 A reference to the *Magnificat* of Mary in the gospel of Luke 1:46–55.

[Antichristus]
        Consummabo uere
            gentem perditionis.
        pro tanto scandalo
            santae religionis.   5
        Ecce superbiam
            humanae potestatis
        teret potentia
            diuinae maiestatis.

Tunc dirigit singulos nuntios ad reges dicens eis.   10

[Antichristus]
        Ite congregantes
            facultates regnorum
        impetu
            furorem superborum.   15

Nuntii uero uenientes coram regibus c[antant].

[Legati Antichristi]
        Ecce noster dominus
            et dues deorum.
        per nos exercitvm   20
            conuocauit suorum.
        Vt per eso teotonicum
            condempnet furorem
        in bello martyrum
            consignabit cruorem.   25

Tunc reges conueniunt ante tronum antichristi. Quibus ille.

[Antichristus]
        Consummabo vere etc.
            [gentem perditionis.
        pro tanto scandalo   30
            santae religionis.

---

14 There is an erasure before *impetu*. Vollmann-Profe suggests that two to three letters are missing in "Tegernseer Ludus de Antichristo," 16.

[ANTICHRIST]
>Verily, I will destroy
>>this people of perdition.
>No hint of scandal will annoy
>>my holiest religion.
>Behold: the puny insolence
>>of human potency
>is vanquished by omnipotence
>>of godly majesty!

Then he sends individual ambassadors to the kings, saying to them:

[ANTICHRIST]
>Go! gather up our forces and
>>bring all kings to our side.
>See that they trample underfoot
>>the madness of such pride!

The messengers accordingly coming to the kings' court[s], s[ing]:

[AMBASSADORS OF ANTICHRIST]
>Behold, our lord the god of gods
>>has given his commission:
>he hereby levies all his hosts
>>to undertake his mission,
>to chastise the Teutonic race
>>and its insane defiance—
>in battle, where your martyrs' blood
>>will witness your compliance.

Then the kings gather before the throne of Antichrist, and he [says] to them:

[ANTICHRIST]
>Verily, I will destroy
>>[this people of perdition.
>No hint of scandal will annoy
>>my holiest religion.

    Ecce superbiam
      humanae potestatis
    teret potentia
      diuinae maiestatis.]
    Ite germaniae   5
      terminos inuadetis
    superbum populum cum
      rege conteretis.

Tunc omnes cantant.

[Reges]   10
    Deus nobiscum est
      quos tuetur potenter
    Pro fide igitur
      pugnemus confidenter.

Et disponentes acies suas in occursum teotonicorum congrediuntur cum eis et supe- 15
ratur ex excitus anitichristi. Tunc rex teotonicorum rediens et sedens in trono suo
cantat.

[Rex Teotonicorum]
    Sanguine patriae
      honor est retinendus.   20
    virtute patriae
      est sanguine uenale.
    sic retinebimus
      decus imperiale.

Tunc ypocrite adducunt claudum coram antichristo. Quo sanato rex teotonicorum 25
hesitabit in fide. Tunc iterum adducent leprosum et illo sanato rex plus dubitabit. Ad
ultimum important feretrum in quo iacebat quidam simulans se in prelio occisum.
Iubet itaque antichristus et surgat dicens.

[Antichristus]
    Signa semper querunt   30
      rudes et infideles

---

16 excitus] Likely *exercitus*

> Behold: the puny insolence
> > of human potency
> is vanquished by omnipotence
> > of godly majesty!]
> Go to the German borders,
> > vanquishing!
> Lay waste that prideful people
> > and their king!

Then they all sing:

[ASSEMBLED KINGS]
> Our God is with us,
> > protecting us with might!
> Therefore in faith
> > we confidently fight!

And ordering their lines of battle, they come together in conflict with the Teutons and the army of Antichrist is overcome. Then the King of the Teutons, returning and sitting on his throne, sings:

[KING OF THE TEUTONS]
> With blood our fatherland is saved,
> > its honor is retained!
> By manly strength our fatherland
> > with blood has been regained!
> So our imperial glory is
> > triumphantly reclaimed!

Then the Hypocrites bring a cripple to the court of Antichrist. When he is cured, the King of the Teutons will be uncertain in his faith. Then again, they will bring a leper and when he is cured the King will doubt even more. And finally they will carry in a bier on which lies someone pretending to have been killed in battle. Accordingly, Antichrist orders that he rise up, saying:

[ANTICHRIST]
> Signs and wonders they will seek,
> > the rude and imbecile.

> surge surge uelocriter quis
> > sim ego reueles.

Tunc ille de feretro cantat.

[SIMULATOR]
> Tu sapientia 5
> > supernae ueritatis
> uirtus inuicta es.
> > diuinae maiestatis.

Et ypocritae secum c[antant].

[SIMULATOR ET YPOCRITAE] 10
> Tu sapientia etc.
> > [supernae ueritatis
> uirtus inuicta es.
> > diuinae maiestatis.]

Tunc rex teotonicorum uidens signum seducitur dicens. 15

[REX TEOTONICORUM]
> Nostro nos impetu semper periclitamur
> aduersus dominum incauti preliamur.
> In huius nomine mortui suscitantur.
> et claudi ambulant. leprosi mundantur. 20
> Illius igitur gloriam ueneremur.

Tunc rex ascendit ad antichristum hoc idem cantat. Cum autem uenerit coram eo flexo genu offert ei coronam c[antat].

[REX TEOTONICORUM]
> Tibi profiteor etc. 25
> > [decus imperiale.
> quo tibi seruiam ius
> > postulo regale.]

Tunc antichristus signans eum et suos in frontibus et imponens ei coronam c[antat].

---

1 *surge* is mistakenly written twice here

> Arise, arise with all due speed,
> and who I am reveal!

Then [the Pretender] sings from the bier:

[PRETENDER]
5
> The wisdom of celestial truth,
> invincible virtue,
> Divinest majesty revealed:
> that's you!

And the Hypocrites joining in [with the Pretender] s[ing]:

10 [PRETENDER AND HYPOCRITES]
> The wisdom [of celestial truth,
> invincible virtue,
> Divinest majesty revealed:
> that's you!]

15 *Then the King of the Teutons, seeing this sign, is led astray, saying:*

[KING OF THE TEUTONS]
> We always seek our peril foolishly!
> We fought against the lord impetuously!
> For in his name the dead become lively!
20
> The lame can walk! There's cure for leprosy!
> We therefore venerate his majesty!

Then the king goes up to Antichrist and he sings this same thing. And when he has come to court, on bended knee he offers him his crown, s[inging]:

[KING OF THE TEUTONS]
25
> To you I profess [publicly
> your might imperial.
> I ask that you accept my service
> to your kingly rule.]

Then Antichrist, signing him and his [men] on the forehead and bestowing on him
30 *the crown, sings:*

[Antichristus]
>   Viue per gratiam etc.
>   [et suscipe honorem
>   dum me recognoscis
>   cunctorum creatorem.] 5

Tunc committit sibi expeditionem ad gentes dicens.

[Antichristus]
>   Vobis credentibus
>   conuertimur ad gentes.

et dato sibi gladio c[antat]. 10
>   Per te disponimus
>   has fieri credentes.

Tunc rex ueniens ad tronum gentilitatis et mittens lengatum ad regem babylonis qui cantat coram eo.

[Legatum] 15
>   Postestas domini
>   maneat in eternum
>   que adoranda est quasi
>   numen sempiternum.
>   Condempnat penitus 20
>   culturam idolorum
>   precipit abici
>   ritus simulacrorum.

Tunc gentilitas ad legatum.

[Gentilitas] 25
>   Finixit inuidia
>   hanc singularitatem.
>   ut unam coloret
>   homo diuinitatem.
>   Ille iure deus 30

---

13 lengatum] Likely *legatum* | **20** Condempnat] Likely *condemnat*

[ANTICHRIST]
    Live through my grace [and you'll receive
        the honor that it brings—
    so long as you acknowledge me
5   creator of all things.]

Then he entrusts to [the King of the Teutons] the campaign against all peoples, saying:

[ANTICHRIST]
    With your belief, we will convert
        the peoples of all lands—

10 *And giving to him a sword, he sings:*
    through you, we'll make believers who
        will cleave to our commands.

Then the King [of the Teutons], coming to the throne of Gentilitas, sends an ambassador [in advance] to the King of Babylon, who sings at his court:[163]

15 [AMBASSADOR]
    The power of the lord remains
        supreme eternally
    and evermore to be adored, the
        only deity.
20   He utterly condemns the worship
        of idolatry
    and orders the rejection of all
        pagan blasphemy.

Then Gentilitas [says] to the ambassador:

25 [GENTILITAS]
    Jealousy has been the cause
        of this bizarre decree,
    that man should worship and revere
        a lone divinity.
30   That lustful god of yours is

---

[163] This suggests that Gentilitas and the King of Babylon must have returned to their original throne after the Emperor's conquest of Jerusalem.

　　　　　　　cupidus estimatur.
　　qui spretus ceteris
　　　　　　　uult ut solus colatur.
　　Nos igitur sequimur
　　　　　　　ritum antiquitatis　　　　　　　　　　　　5
　　diis discrimina
　　　　　　　reddimus deitatis.

Tunc nuntius.

[Nuntius]
　　　　　　　Vnus est dominus　　　　　　　　　　　　　10
　　　　　　　　　quem iure ueneramur
　　　　　　　qui solus deus et.

et deitiens simulacrum c[antat].

　　　　　　　ydolum detestamur.

Statim gentiles concurrent. et preliantur cum exercitu antichrist. et superatus rex 15
babylonis ducitur captiuus ad antichristum. Tunc rex genu flexo offert coronam antichristo d[icens].

[Rex Babylonis]
　　　　　　　Tibi profiteor etc.
　　　　　　　　　[decus imperiale.　　　　　　　　　　　20
　　　　　　　quo tibi seruiam ius
　　　　　　　　　postulo regale.]

Tunc antichristus signans eum et suos in frontibus et imponens coronam ei c[antat].

[Antichristus]
　　　　　　　Viue per gratiam etc.　　　　　　　　　　　25
　　　　　　　　　[et suscipe honorem
　　　　　　　dum me recognoscis
　　　　　　　　　cunctorum creatorem.]

> very rightly to be feared
> if, in contempt for other gods,
> > he seeks to be revered.
> We follow therefore all our
> > ancient rites
> Each several god receives from us
> > his rights.

Then the ambassador [sings]:

[AMBASSADOR]
> One is our lord, whom
> > rightly we adore,
> He who alone is god.

And throwing down an idol he s[ings]:

> This idol we deplore!

Immediately, the Gentiles rush in to battle and fight against the army of Antichrist. And the King of Babylon is overcome and led a captive to Antichrist. Then the King on bended knee offers the crown to Antichrist, saying:

[KING OF BABYLON]
> To you I profess [publicly
> > your might imperial.
> I ask that you accept my service
> > to your kingly rule.]

Then Antichrist, signing him and his [men] on their foreheads and bestowing the crown on him, s[ings]:

[ANTICHRIST]
> Live through my grace [and you'll receive
> > the honor that it brings—
> So long as you acknowledge me
> > creator of all things.]

Statim redeunt ad sedes suas cantantes omnes.

[OMNES]
   Omnium rectorem
     te solum profitemur.
   tibi tota mente   5
     semper obsequemur.

Tunc antichristus dirigens ypocritas ad synagogam c[antat].

[ANTICHRISTUS]
   Iudeis dicite
     messim aduenisse.   10
   et me in gentibus
     tributum accepisse.
   Iudeis dicite
     en ego sum messyas.
   ego sum promissus   15
     eis per prophetas.

Tunc ypocrite ad synagogam.

[YPOCRITAE]
   Regalis gneris
     gens est peculiaris.   20
   fidelis populus
     ubique predicans.
   Pro tuenda lege
     iam dudum exulasti
   procul a patria   25
     messiam exspectasti.
   hec exspectatio
     reddet hereditatem.
   iocunda nouitas
     mutabit uetustatem.   30
   Ecce mysterium
     tuae redemptionis.

---

1 cantantes omnes] Likely meant to read *omnes cantantes* following scribal marks ("//") above the two words indicating they should be switched. See also Vollmann-Profe, "Tegernseer Ludus de Antichristo," 18 | **19** gneris] Likely *generis*

Immediately, they all return to their seats, singing:

[ALL]
>That you alone rule everyone
>>we publicly admit!
>To you alone, with all our might,
>>we always will submit!

The Antichrist, sending Hypocrisy to Synagoga, s[ings]:

[ANTICHRIST]
>Go to the Jews and say to them
>>that their Messiah's come,
>that all the peoples of the world
>>pay tribute and succumb.
>Go to the Jews and say to them:
>>Messiah—look, it's me!
>I am the one who's promised you
>>by ancient prophecy!

Then the Hypocrites [go] to Synagoga:

[HYPOCRITES]
>A royal people set apart:
>>you are the chosen race.
>As faithful people you have been
>>proclaimed in every place.
>For keeping to the law you've long
>>been exiled, slain, pariahs—
>far from your fatherland, you wait
>>the coming of Messiah.
>This waiting will be recompensed
>>to your posterity:
>a new and joyful time will heal
>>your old adversity!
>Behold, redemption is at hand,
>>behold the mystery:

>   rex enim natus est
>   auctor religionis.
>   Hic est emmanueal
>   quem testantur scripture
>   per cuius gratiam 5
>   tu regnabis secure.
>   Erexit humiles.
>   et superbos deiecit.
>   potenter omnia
>   sub pedibus subiecit. 10
>   Surge ierusalem
>   surge illuminare.
>   captiua diu
>   synagoga letare.

Tunc synagoga. 15

[Synagoga]
>   Hec consolatio
>   diuinae bonitatis.
>   laborem respicit
>   nostrae captiuitatis. 20
>   Eamus igitur
>   obuiam saluatori.
>   dignum est reddere
>   gloriam redemptori.

Tunc synagoga sugens uadit ad antichristum et cetera. 25

[Synagoga]
>   Ades emanuel
>   quem semper ueneramur
>   in cuius gloria
>   nos quoque gloriamur. 30

Tunc uenientem suscipit synagogam signans eam et dicens.

a king is born to lead your faith
         in full authority!
This king is the Emmanuel
         as witnessed by scripture
5 and through his grace you'll reign with him
         and always be secure.
He raises up the humble,
         the proud he will defeat.[164]
With power, everything is cast
10   down underneath his feet.
Arise, Jerusalem!
         Arise and shine![165]
Rejoice, O captive Synagogue!
         It's time!

15 *Then Synagoga:*

[SYNAGOGA]
         This is the consolation of
                  God's generosity,
         rewarding us for all the years
20   of our captivity.
         Let's go, therefore, and meet him now—
                  the savior promised us!
         It's right to offer praise to the
                  redeemer glorious!

25 *Then Synagoga rises and goes out to Antichrist and the rest:*

[SYNAGOGA]
         You come, Emmanuel—
                  whom we have waited for,
         whom we will always glorify
30   and whom we all adore.

Then, when Synagoga comes, [Antichrist] receives her and, signing her [with his mark], sings:

---

164 Another reference to the *Magnificat*.
165 Paraphrase of Isaiah 60:1.

[ANTICHRISTUS]
>> Per me egredere
>> > uectem confusionis.
>> tibi restituo
>> > terram promissionis.
>> In tuo lumine
>> > en gentes ambulant.
>> et sub pacis tuae
>> > lege reges regnabunt.

Tunc synagoga redeunte. intrant prophetae dicentes.

[ENOCH ET HELIAM]
>> Verbum patris habens diuinitatem.
>> in uirgine sumpsit humanitatem.
>> manens deus effectus est mortalis.
>> semper deus. factus est temporalis.
>> Non naturae usu sictestante.
>> hoc factum est sed deo imperante
>> nostram sumpsit infirmitatem.
>> ut infirmis conferret firmitatem.
>> hunc iudei mortalem cognoucrunt
>> immortalem quem esse nesci erunt.
>> nec sermoni nec signis credidere.
>> sub pilator christum crucifixere.
>> Moriendo mortem mortificauit.
>> a gehenna credentes liberauit.
>> Hic surrexit uere non moriturus.
>> regnat semper in proximo uenturus.
>> Hic seculum per ignem iudicabit.
>> uniuersos in carne suscitabit.
>> A reprobis saluandos separabit.
>> malos dampnans. bonos glorificabit.
>> Vere scitis quid scripture loquantur.

---

28 iudicabit] Originally: *iudicauit*; though, a later hand corrected the word to *iudicabit*

[ANTICHRIST]
    Through me, the end of darkness
        is at hand.
    To you I will restore
5   the promised land.
    Your light will all the people's way
        make plain.[166]
    In peace, and by your laws,
        all kings will reign.

10 *Then as Synagoga returns, the prophets [Enoch and Elijah] enter, saying:*[167]

[ENOCH AND ELIJAH]
    The Father's word, having divinity,
    in Virgin's womb took on humanity.
    Remaining God, He took mortality:
15   eternal God in temporality!
    And not by Nature's custom was this done,
    but by the Lordly will of God alone.
    So He took on our incapacities
    to strengthen mankind with His constancy.
20   The Jews believed in His mortality
    but would not recognize Divinity;
    both miracles and teachings they denied
    and under Pilate, Christ was crucified.
    His dying dealt to Death its own death blow
25   and freed all true believers from below.
    He truly rose and will not die again.
    He lives and when He comes will always reign!
    This generation He will judge with fire:
    the dead will be raised up by His desire!
30   The sinners from the saved He will divide:
    the wicked damned, the righteous glorified!
    Believe the truth the Scriptures testify:

---

166 This is a sinister reference to Ephesians 4:17, in which "the people walk in vanity" (*gentes ambulant in vanitate*).

167 Enoch and Elijah are the only characters specifically instructed in the text to speak (*dicere*) most of their lines, rather than to sing (*cantare*) them.

Enoch uiuum et Heliam testantur.

Tunc synagoga.

[SYNAGOGA]
    Vbinam sunt?

Illi. 5

[ENOCH ET HELIAS]
    Nos sumus
        uere
    in quos fines
        seculorum deuenere. 10

[ENOCH]
    Iste Enoch.

[HELIAS]
        et ego
    sum Helias. 15

[ENOCH ET HELIAS]
    quos hucusque serua
        uerat messias.
    qui iam uenit.
        et adhuc est uenturus. 20
    per nos primum
        israel redempturus.
    Ecce uenit
        homo perditionis.
    magnae consummans 25
        muros babylonis.
    Non est christus.

that Enoch and Elijah are alive![168]

Then Synagoga:

[SYNAGOGA]
    And where are they?

They [say]:

[ENOCH AND ELIJAH]
        That's us!
           Truly!
        Through us the end of time
           has come to be!

[ENOCH]
        I'm Enoch.

[ELIJAH]
           Yes, and me—
        well ... I'm Elijah.

[ENOCH AND ELIJAH]
        We've waited all this time
           for the Messiah
        who came before and soon
           will come again.
        But first, through us, Israel
           will be redeemed!
        Behold, he's come:
           the man of perdition[169]
        who razes flat
           the walls of Babylon!
        He is not Christ!

---

168 This speech is a close paraphrase of the Apostles' Creed.

169 A reference to 2 Thessalonians 2:3–4: "Let not one deceive you in any way; for that day will come ... and the son of perdition, who opposes and exalts himself against every other so-called god or object of worship, so that he takes his seat in the temple of God, proclaiming himself to be God."

Tunc tollunt ei uelum. Statim synagoga conuertitur ad uerba prophetarum dicens.

[Synagoga]
        Seducti sumus uere
            per antichristum
        qui mentitur se   5
            iudeorum christum.
        Certa iuditia sunt
            nostrae libertatis.
        helyas. et enoch
            prophetae ueritatis.   10
        Tibi gratias damus
            adonay rex gloriae.
        personarum trinitatis
            eiusdem substantiae.
        Vere pater deus est.   15
            cuius unigenitus deus est.
        idem deus est
            amborum spiritus.

Interim ypocritae uenientes ad antichristum c[antantes].

[Ypocritae]   20
        O culmen regium
            diuinae maiestatis
        tibi subtrahitur
            honor diuinitatis
        intrauere senes   25
            doctores uanitatis.
        qui blasphemant tuae
            honorem potestatis.
        Iudeis predicant

Then they remove her veil.[170] *Immediately, Synagoga is converted by the words of the prophets, saying:*

[SYNAGOGA]

  Truly, we were led astray
    and this is Antichrist
  who lied to us and said he was
    the Jews' own promised Christ!
  Now here are the authentic proofs
    of our new liberty:
  Elijah, Enoch—prophets who
    have spoken truthfully!
  To you we give our grateful thanks,
    O Adonai, our King:
  a Trinity of Persons but
    in essence One Being.
  Truly, God the Father, from Whom
    issues God the Son,
  and from both come the Spirit so
    that God is Three in One.[171]

Meanwhile, the Hypocrites come to Antichrist, s[inging]:

[HYPOCRITES]

  O highest of all kingly kings,
    divinest majesty!
  From you has honor been removed—
    from your divinity!
  Old men have come upon the scene:
    teachers of falsity,
  who denigrate your honor and
    who utter blasphemy!
  They're preaching to the Jews just like

---

170 Wright misinterprets the text here, translating *Tunc tollunt ei uelum* as "Then they strip off Antichrist's mask." This is an error that causes great confusion, and Wright himself acknowledged that it could refer to Synagoga's veil: *The Play of Antichrist*, 95 and n. 72. Nowhere in the play is Antichrist described as masked.
171 The converted Synagoga's confession of the Christian faith is carefully worded to align with the Roman Church's doctrine of the Trinity.

        tenore scripturarum.
    te rex omnipotens
        caput ypocritarum.

Tunc antichristus ad ypocritas.

[ANTICHRISTUS]   5
    Cum me totus orbis
        studeat adorare.
    ius mei nominis quis
        audeat negare.
    Synagogam et senes   10
        mihi representate.
    reos conueniam
        super hac leuitate.

Tunc ministri uenientes ad prophetas et synagogam c[antantes].

[MINISTRI ANTICHRISTI]   15
    Testes mendatii
        precones falsitatis
    uos tribunal uocat
        diuinae maiestatis.

Tunc prophete.   20

[ENOCH ET HELIAS]
    Non seducet homo
        iniquitatis
    seruo christi ministris
        falsitatis.   25

Tunc nuntii adducunt prophetas et synagogam ad antichristum. Quibus ille.

[ANTICHRISTUS]
    Fert in insaniam
        proprietatis uos.
    quos decipiunt   30
        uultus auctoritatis.
    Sanctis promissus sum

        the scriptures prophesy;
    they're calling you, all-knowing king,
        King of Hypocrisy!

Then Antichrist [says] to the Hypocrites:

5 [ANTICHRIST]
    When all the world is mine alone
        and all men worship me,
    who dares to contradict my law
        and my authority?
10   Seize Synagogue and those old men
        and bring them here to me,
    and I will make them sorry for
        their grievous perfidy.

Then ministers [of Antichrist], coming to the prophets and Synagoga, s[ing]:

15 [MINISTERS OF ANTICHRIST]
    You witnesses of filthy lies,
        mouths of mendacity,
    you're called to the tribunal of
        divinest majesty.

20 *Then the prophets [sing]:*

[ENOCH AND ELIJAH]
    He will not lead us far astray,
        that evil man of sin—
    Christ's servants, we reject as false
25   the service you are in.

Then the messengers lead the prophets and Synagoga to Antichrist. He says to them:

[ANTICHRIST]
    Appearances have carried you
        into insanity.
30   You've been deceived by semblances,
        by false authority.
    I am the one who's coming's promised

　　　　　　redemptio futura
　　　　uere messias ut
　　　　　　testatur scriptura.
　　　　De me suscipite
　　　　　　formam religionis.   5
　　　　sum infidelibus
　　　　　　lapis offensionis.

Tunc prophetae.

[Enoch et Helias]
　　　　Tu blasphemus   auctor iniquitatis.   10
　　　　radix mali.   turbator ueritatis.
　　　　antichristus   seductor pietatis.
　　　　uere mendax   sub forma pietatis.

Tunc antichristus commotus dicit ministris.

[Antichristus]   15
　　　　　　Ecce blasphemias
　　　　　　　　meae diuinitatis.
　　　　　　ulciscatur manus
　　　　　　　　diuinae maiestatis.
　　　　　　qui blasphemant in me   20
　　　　　　　　diuinam pietatem.
　　　　　　diuini numinis
　　　　　　　　gustent seueritatem.
　　　　　　Pereant penitus
　　　　　　　　oues occisionis   25
　　　　　　pro tanto scandalo
　　　　　　　　sanctae religionis.

Tandem synagoga c[antat] confessionem istam.

[Synagoga]
　　　　　　Nos erroris penitet.   30
　　　　　　　　ad fidem conuertimur.

to the saints to be:
the true messiah! All the scriptures
testify to me.
Receive from me the rule of the
religion I compel.
For I am he, the stumbling-block
of every infidel.[172]

Then the prophets say:

[ENOCH AND ELIJAH]
You blasphemer! Font of iniquity!
You root of evil! Truth's adversary!
You Antichrist: seducing piety
and lying in the form of piety!

The Antichrist, enraged, says to his ministers:

[ANTICHRIST]
Listen to these blasphemers
of my divinity!
They'll be avenged by might of my
divine hand's majesty!
All those who blaspheme thus against
my godly piety
will taste, with all my might divine,
a just severity.
Like sheep led to the slaughter,[173] they
will perish in derision
for bringing such a scandal on
this holiest religion.

Finally, Synagoga s[ings] this confession:

[SYNAGOGA]
Our many errors we repent,
for now our faith is sure.

---
172 Cf. Isaiah 8:14.
173 A reference to Isaiah 53:7, which Christians interpret as a reference to Jesus.

>   quicquid nobis inferet
>   persecutor patimur.

Tunc ministri educunt eos et occidunt. Interim vero dum occiduntur. ecclesia c[antat].

[ECCLESIA]
>   Fasciculus mirrae dilectus meus mihi.   5

Tunc ministris reuersis. antichristus dirigit nuntios suos ad singulos reges. c[antantes].

[ANTICHRISTUS]
>   Reges conueniant.
>   et agmina sanctorum.   10
>   adorari uolo
>   a gloria regnorum.
>   Cuncta diuinitus
>   manus ima firmauit.
>   suos diuinitas   15
>   hostes exterminauit.
>   Pace conclusa sunt
>   cuncta iura regnorum
>   ad coronam uocat
>   suos deus deorum.   20

Tunc omnes reges conueniunt undique cum suis usque ad presentiam antichristi.

[REGES]
>   Cuncta diuinitus etc.
>   manus ima firmauit.
>   suos diuinitas   25
>   hostes exterminauit.
>   Pace conclusa sunt
>   cuncta iura regnorum

> Whatever persecution comes
> to us, we will endure.

Then the ministers lead them [Synagoga and the prophets] out and kill them. Meanwhile, even as they are being killed, Ecclesia s[ings]:

5 [ECCLESIA]
> A bundle of myrrh is my well-beloved unto me.[174]

Then as the ministers return, Antichrist sends his ambassadors to the individual kings, s[inging]:

[ANTICHRIST]
10
> Go out: collect the kings,
> the holy multitudes.
> I wish to be adored
> in royal magnitude.
> All things the hand of god
15
> has fortified below
> and all his enemies
> divinity lays low.
> In peace, the laws of kings
> are brought to one accord.
20
> The god of gods now calls
> his people to his sword.

Then all the kings come together from every place with their [men], and then into the presence of Antichrist:

[KINGS]
25
> All things the hand of god
> has fortified below
> and all his enemies
> divinity lays low.
> In peace, the laws of kings
30
> are brought to one accord.

---

174 A direct quotation from the Song of Songs 1:13. Many later medieval motets were composed around this text, and it is possible that the playwright intended Synagoga to sing not only this verse but others, as appropriate.

>   ad coronam uocat
>   suos deus deorum.

Quibus antichristus.

[Antichristus]
>   Ista predixerunt   5
>   mei predicatores.
>   uiri mei nominis
>   et iuris cultores.
>   Hec mea gloria
>   quam diu predixere.   10
>   qua fruentur mecum
>   quicumque meruere.
>   Post eorum casum
>   quos uanitas illusit.
>   pax et securitas   15
>   uniuersa conclusit.

Statim fit sonitus super caput antichristi. et eo corruente. et omnibus suis fugientibus. ecclesia cantat.

[Ecclesia]
>   Ecce homo qui non posuit deum adiutorem suum.   20
>   ego autem sicut oliua fructifera in domo dei.

Tunc omnibus redeuntibus ad fidem. ecclesia ipsos suscipiens incipit.

[Ecclesia]
>   **Laudem dicite deo nostro. [omnes sancti eius,**
>   **et qui timetis Deum, pusilli et magni:**   25
>   **quoniam regnavit Dominus Deus noster omnipotens.**
>   **Gaudeamus et exsultemus et demus gloriam ei.**
>   **Genus electum, gens sancta, populus acquisitionis**
>   **memores memorum laudate Deum.**
>   **Gloria Patri et Filio et Spiritui Sancto.]**   30

> The god of gods now calls
> his people to his sword.

Antichrist s[ays] to them:

[ANTICHRIST]
> These things have all been prophesied
> by those who preach for me:
> all men obey my royal name
> and my authority.
> This is my glory, which has long
> been prophesied to me,
> which everyone who merits it
> will share abundantly.
> After the fall of those who were
> deceived by vanity,
> all things will now be done in peace,
> in my security.

Immediately, there should be a crash above the head of Antichrist, causing him to fall down and all of his [men] to flee. Ecclesia sings:

[ECCLESIA]
> Behold the man who made not God his strength.
> But I am like an olive tree in the house of God.[175]

Then all return to the faith. And Ecclesia, receiving them, begins:

[ECCLESIA]
> **Speak praise to Our God, [all you His saints**
> **and whoever fears God, both tiny and great:**
> **because Our God reigns, omnipotent.**
> **Let us rejoice and exult and give Him glory.**
> **O chosen race, O holy nation, O people of His own,**
> **remembering His memorable deeds, praise God.**
> **Glory be to the Father, and to the Son, and to the Holy Spirit.]**[176]

---

175 A direct quotation from Psalm 52:7a, 8a.
176 A creative quotation and use of materials from Revelation 19 and 1 Peter 2:9.

Bibliography

Primary Sources

Adso of Montier-en-Der. *Epistola Adsonis ad Gerbergam reginam de ortu et tempore antichristi* [Letter on the Origin and Time of the Antichrist]. In *Apocalyptic Spirituality: Treatises and Letter of Lactantius, Adso of Montier-en-Der, Joachim of Fiore, the Spiritual Franciscans, Savonarola*, translated by Bernard McGinn, 89–96. New York: Paulist Press, 1979.

Bede the Venerable. *Libri II: De arte metrica et De schematibus et tropis = The art of poetry and rhetoric*. Translated and edited by Calvin B. Kendall. Saarbrücken: AQ-Verlag, 1991.

Benedict of Nursia. *The Rule of Saint Benedict in English*. Translated by Timothy Fry. Collegeville: Liturgical Press, 1982.

Benedict of Nursia. *La règle de Saint Benoît*, ed. A. de Vogüé and J. Neufville. 3 vols. Paris: Éditions du Cerf, 1972.

Brecht, Bertolt. *Brecht on Theatre: The Development of an Aesthetic*. Edited and translated by John Willet. New York: Hill and Wang, 1964.

Carmen de gestis Frederici I imperatoris in Lombardia. Translated by Thomas Carson. New York: Italica Press, 1994.

Froumund of Tegernsee. *Codex Epistolarum Tegernseensium (Froumund)*. MGH Epp. sel. 3. Edited by Karl Strecker. Berlin: Weidmannsche Buchhandlung, 1925.

Gerhoh of Reichersberg. *Commentarius in Psalmos*. MGH Ldl 3. Hannover: Hahnsche Buchhandlung, 1897.

Gerhoh of Reichersberg. *De investigatione Antichristi*. MGH Ldl 3. Hannover: Hahnsche Buchhandlung, 1897.

Gregory VII. *Registrum Gregorii*. MGH Epp. Edited by Erich Casper. Berlin: Weidmannsche Buchhandlung, 1920.

Honorius Augustodunensis. *Gemma animae*. Edited by J. P. Migne. *Patrologia Latina*. Vol. 172. Paris: Garnier Fratres, 1895.

Liber Pontificalis. Edited by Louis Marie Olivier Duchesne. 2 vols. Paris: Ernest Thorin, 1892.

Ludus de Antichristo. In *The Drama of the Medieval Church*, edited by Karl Young. Vol. 2, 369–96. Oxford: Clarendon Press, 1933.

Ludus de Antichristo. In "Antichrist and Adam: Two Mediaeval Religious Dramas," translated by William H. Hulme. *Western Reserve University Bulletin* 28.8 (August 1925): 5–32.

Ludus de Antichristo. In *The Play of Antichrist*, translated by John Wright. Toronto: Pontifical Institute of Mediaeval Studies, 1967.

Ludus de Antichristo. Latin edition and German translation by Gisela Vollmann-Profe. Göppingen: Kümmerle, 1981.

Ludus de Nativitate. In *Medieval Drama*, edited and translated by David Bevington, 178–201. Boston: Houghton Mifflin, 1975.

Ludus de Passione. In *Medieval Drama*, edited and translated by David Bevington, 203–23. Boston: Houghton Mifflin, 1975.

Müller, Ulrich, ed. *Kreuzzugsdichtung*. Deutsche Texte 9. Tübingen: M. Niemeyer, 1969.

Ordo prophetarum. Edited by Karl Young. Madison: Wisconsin Academy of Sciences, Arts and Letters, 1922.

Ordo Romanus Primus. Edited by Vernon Staley. London: De La More Press, 1905.

Otto of Freising and Rahewin. *Ottonis et Rahewini Gesta Friderici I Imperatoris*. MGH SS rer. Germ 46. Edited by Adolf Hofmeister. Hannover and Leipzig: Hahnsche Buchhandlung, 1912.

Otto of Freising and Rahewin. *The Deeds of Frederick Barbarossa*. Translated and edited by Charles Christopher Mierow. New York: Columbia University Press, 2004.

Otto of Freising and Rahewin. *The Two Cities: A Chronicle of Universal History to the Year 1146 A.D.* Translated by Charles Christopher Mierow. Edited by Austin P. Evans and Charles Knapp. New York: Octagon Books, 1966.

Die Tegernseer Briefsammlung des 12. Jahrhunderts. MGH, Briefe d. dt. Kaiserzeit 2. Edited by Helmut Plechl, 1–341. Hannover: Hahnsche Buchhandlung, 2002.

Thietmar of Merseburg. *Chronicon*. MGH SS rer. Germ. [N.S.] 9. Edited by Robert Holtzmann. Berlin: Weidmannsche Buchhandlung, 1935.

Secondary Sources

Aebischer, Pascale. "Didascalia and Speech in Dramatic Text." *Journal of Dramatic Theory and Criticism* 17.2 (Spring 2003): 25–44.

Ahn, Dongmyung. "The Exegetical Function of the Conductus in MS Egerton 2615." PhD diss., City University of New York, 2018.

Akbari, Suzanne Conklin. *Seeing through the Veil: Optical Theory and Medieval Allegory*. Toronto: University of Toronto, 2004.

Arlt, Wulf. *Ein Festoffozium des Mittelalters aus Beauvais in seiner liturgischen und musikalischen Bedeutung*. Cologne: Arno Volk Verlag, 1970.

Arnold, Benjamin. *Medieval Germany, 500–1300: A Political Interpretation*. Toronto: University of Toronto Press, 1997.

Arnold, Benjamin. *Power and Property in Medieval Germany: Economic and Social Change ca. 900–1300*. Oxford: Oxford University Press, 2004.

Arnold, Benjamin. *Princes and Territories in Medieval Germany*. Cambridge: Cambridge University Press, 1991.

Aronson-Lehavi, Sharon. *Street Scenes: Late Medieval Acting and Performance*. New York: Palgrave Macmillan, 2011.

Axton, Richard. *European Drama of the Early Middle Ages*. Pittsburgh: University of Pittsburgh Press, 1975.

Backhouse, Janet. *The Sherborne Missal*. Toronto: University of Toronto Press, 1999.

Baird, Joseph L. *The Personal Correspondence of Hildegard of Bingen*. New York: Oxford University Press, 2006.

Bamberg, Michael. "Narrative Discourse and Identities." In *Narratology Beyond Literary Criticism*, edited by Jan Christoph Meister, Tom Kindt, and Wilhelm Schernus, 213–38. Berlin: Walter de Gruyter, 2005.

Baumgaertner, Jill. "The Benediktbeuern 'Ludus de Nativitate': Journey to Fulfillment." *Christianity and Literature* (1979): 13–30.

Bazerman, Charles. "Textual Performance: Where the Action at a Distance Is." *JAC* 23.2 (2003): 379–96.

Bedos-Rezak, Brigitte Miriam. "Civic Liturgies and Urban Records in Northern France, 1100–1400." In *City and Spectacle in Medieval Europe*, edited by Barbara Hanawalt and Kathryn Reyerson, 34–55. Minneapolis: University of Minnesota Press, 1994.

Bedos-Rezak, Brigitte Miriam. "Seals and Stars: Law, Magic and the Bureaucratic Process (Twelfth-

Thirteenth Centuries)." In *Seals and their Context in the Middle Ages*, edited by Phillip R. Schofield, 89–100. Philadelphia: Oxbow, 2015.
Bedos-Rezak, Brigitte Miriam. *When Ego Was Imago: Signs of Identity in the Middle Ages*. Edited by Eva Frojmovic. Boston: Brill, 2011.
Bevington, David. *Medieval Drama*. Boston: Houghton Mifflin, 1975.
Bisson, Thomas N. *The Crisis of the Twelfth Century: Power, Lordship and the Origins of European Government*. Princeton: Princeton University Press, 2009.
Blau, Herbert. *The Audience*. Baltimore: Johns Hopkins University Press, 1990.
Blumenthal, Uta-Renate. *The Investiture Controversy: Church and Monarchy from the Ninth to the Twelfth Century*. Philadelphia: University of Pennsylvania Press, 1988.
Brown, Warren C., Marios Costambeys, Matthew Innes, and Adam J. Kosto, eds. *Documentary Culture and the Laity in the Early Middle Ages*. Cambridge: Cambridge University Press, 2013.
Bruce, Scott G. *Silence and Sign Language in Medieval Monasticism: The Cluniac Tradition, ca. 900–1200*. Cambridge: Cambridge University Press, 2007.
Brunner, Otto. *Land und Herrschaft: Grundfragen der territorialen Verfassungsgeschichte Südostdeutschlands im Mittelalter*. Brünn: Roher, 1943.
Burrow, J. A. *Gestures and Looks in Medieval Narrative*. Cambridge: Cambridge University Press, 2002.
Butterworth, Philip, ed. *The Narrator, the Expositor, and the Prompter in European Medieval Theatre*. Turnhout: Brepols, 2007.
Buttinger, Sabine. *Das Kloster Tegernsee und sein Beziehungsgefüge im 12. Jahrhundert*. Munich: Verlag des Vereins für Diözesangeschichte von München und Freising, 2004.
Booker, Courtney M. *Past Convictions: The Penance of Louis the Pious and the Decline of the Carolingians*. Philadelphia: University of Pennsylvania Press, 2009.
Bouchard, Constance B. "'Feudalism,' Cluny, and the Investiture Controversy." In *Medieval Monks and Their World: Ideas and Realities*, edited by David Blanks, Michael Frassetto, and Amy Livingstone, 81–91. Boston: Brill, 2006.
Bourgeault, Cynthia. "Liturgical Dramaturgy." *Comparative Drama* 17.2 (Summer 1983): 124–40.
Boynton, Susan. *Shaping a Monastic Identity: Liturgy and History at the Imperial Abbey of Farfa, 1000–1125*. Ithaca: Cornell University Press, 2006.
Candy, Linda, Ernest Edmonds and Craig Vear. "Practice-Based Research." In *The Routledge International Handbook of Practice-Based Research*, edited by Craig Vear, 1–15. New York: Routledge, 2021.
Chambers, E. K. *The Mediaeval Stage*. 2 vols. Oxford: Oxford University Press, 1903.
Cillers, Johan. "Liturgy as a Space for Anticipation." *HTS Teologiese Studies/Theological Studies* 67.2 (2011): 1–7.
Clanchy, M. T. *From Memory to Written Record: England 1066–1307*. 3rd edition. Oxford: Basil Blackwell, 2012.
Clanchy, M. T. "Medieval Mentalities and Primitive Legal Practice." *Law, Laity and Solidarities: Essays in Honour of Susan Reynolds*. Edited by Pauline Stafford, Janet L. Nelson, and Jane Martindale. Manchester: Manchester University Press, 2001.
Classen, Peter. *Gerhoch von Reichersberg: Eine Biographie*. Wiesbaden: Franz Steiner, 1960.
Clopper, Lawrence M. *Drama, Play, and Game: English Festive Culture in the Medieval and Early Modern Period*. Chicago: University of Chicago Press, 2001.
Cohen, Jeremy. "*Synagoga conversa*: Honorius Augustodunensis, the Song of Songs, and Christianity's 'Eschatological Jew'." *Speculum* 79.2 (April 2004): 309–40.
Conner, Patrick W. *Anglo-Saxon Exeter: A Tenth-Century Cultural History*. Rochester: Boydell Press, 1993.
Constable, Giles. "Dictators and Diplomats in the Eleventh and Twelfth Centuries: Medieval

Epistolography and the Birth of Modern Bureaucracy." *Dumbarton Oaks Papers* 46, *Homo Byzantinus: Papers in Honor of Alexander Kazhdan* (1992): 37–46.
Constable, Giles. *The Reformation of the Twelfth Century*. Cambridge: Cambridge University Press, 1996.
Constable, Giles. "Renewal and Reform in Religious Life: Concepts and Realities." *Renaissance and Renewal in the Twelfth Century*, edited by Robert Louis Benson and Giles Constable with Carol D. Lanham, 37–67. Toronto: University of Toronto Press, 1991.
Cowdrey, H. E. J. *The Cluniacs and the Gregorian Reform*. Oxford: Oxford University Press, 1970.
Crane, Susan A. *Collecting and Historical Consciousness in Early Nineteenth-Century Germany*. Ithaca: Cornell University Press, 2000.
Cushing, Kathleen G. "Law and Disputation in Eleventh-Century *Libelli de lite*." In *The Use of Canon Law in Ecclesiastical Administration, 1000–1234*, edited by Melodie H. Eichbauer and Danica Summerlin, 185–94. Boston: Brill, 2019.
Dalmais, Irénée Henri. "Theology of the Liturgical Celebration." In *The Church at Prayer: Principles of the Liturgy*, edited by Aimé Georges Martimont et al., 1: 227–80. 4 vols. Collegeville, Minnesota: Liturgical Press, 1987.
Dey, Hendrick. "From 'Street' to 'Piazza': Urban Politics, Public Ceremony, and the Redefinition of *platea* in Communal Italy and Beyond." *Speculum* 91.4 (October 2016): 919–44.
DiCesare, Michelina. "The Eschatological Meaning of the *Templum Domini* (the Dome of the Rock) in Jerusalem." *Aevum* 88.2 (May–August 2014): 311–29.
Dienst, Heide. *Regionalgeschichte und Gesellschaft im Hochmittelalter am Beispiel Österreichs*. Vienna: Böhlau, 1990.
Doig, Allan. *Liturgy and Architecture: From the Early Church to the Middle Ages*. New York: Routledge, 2016.
Dox, Donalee. *The Idea of the Theater in Latin Christian Thought*. Ann Arbor: University of Michigan Press, 2004.
Dronke, Peter. *Nine Medieval Latin Plays*. New York: Cambridge University Press, 1994.
Drumbl, Johann. "Revisiting the Plays of the Codex Buranus." In *Revisiting the Codex Buranus: Contents, Contexts, Compositions*, edited by Tristan E. Franklinos and Henry Hope, 227–50. Studies in Medieval and Renaissance Music 21. Woodbridge: Boydell & Brewer, 2020.
Emmerson, Richard K., and Ronald B. Herzman. *The Apocalyptic Imagination in Medieval Literature*. Philadelphia: University of Pennsylvania Press, 1992.
Enders, Jody. "Critical Stages." *Theatre Survey* 50.2 (November 2009): 317–25.
Enders, Jody. *The Medieval Theater of Cruelty: Rhetoric, Memory, Violence*. Ithaca: Cornell University Press, 1999.
Enders, Jody. *Murder by Accident: Medieval Theater, Modern Media, Critical Intentions*. Chicago: University of Chicago Press, 2009.
Enders, Jody. *Rhetoric and the Origins of Medieval Drama*. Ithaca: Cornell University Press, 1992.
Engelhardt, Johann Georg Veit. *Dies memoriae Jesu Christi vitae restituti pie celebrandos: Disseritur de ludo paschali saeculi duodecimi qui inscriptus est: De adventu et interitu Antichristi*. Erlangen: Typis Jugeanis, 1831.
Fabre, Martine. *Sceau médiéval: Analyse d'une pratique culturelle*. Paris: L'Harmattan, 2001.
Fasoli, Gina. "Friedrich Barbarossa und die lombardischen Städte." *Friedrich Barbarossa*. Edited by Gunther Wolf. Darmstadt: Wissenschaftliche Buchgesellschaft, 1975.
Fassler, Margot. *Gothic Song: Victorine Sequences and Augustinian Reform in Twelfth-Century Paris*. New York: Cambridge University Press, 1993.
Fassler, Margot. "Liturgy and Sacred History in the Twelfth-Century Tympana at Chartres." *Art Bulletin* 75.3 (September 1993): 499–520.

Fassler, Margot. "The Meaning of Entrance: Liturgical Commentaries and the Introit Tropes." In *Reflections on the Sacred: A Musicological Perspective*, edited by Paul Brainard, 8–18. Yale Studies in Sacred Music, Worship and the Arts.New Haven: Yale Institute of Sacred Music, 1994.

Fassler, Margot. *The Virgin of Chartres: Making History through Liturgy and the Arts*. New Haven: Yale University Press, 2010.

Fassler, Margot and Rebecca A. Baltzer, eds. *The Divine Office in the Latin Middle Ages: Methodology and Source Studies, Regional Developments, Hagiography*. New York: Oxford University Press, 2000.

Ferzoco, George and Carolyn Muessig, eds. *Medieval Monastic Education*. New York: Leicester University Press, 2000.

Fichte, J. O. *Expository Voices in Medieval Drama*. Nürnberg: H. Carl, 1975.

Fischer, Hans. *Katalog der Handschriften der Universitätsbibliothek Erlangen*. 6 vols. Erlangen: Erlangen University Library, 1928.

Flanigan, C. Clifford. "The Roman Rite and the Origins of the Liturgical Drama." *University of Toronto Quarterly* 43.3 (Spring 1974): 263–84.

Flanigan, C. Clifford. "The Moving Subject: Medieval Liturgical Processions in Semiotic and Cultural Perspective." In *Moving Subjects: Processional Performance in the Middle Ages and the Renaissance*, edited by Kathleen Ashley and Wim Hüsken, 35–51. Ludus 5. Atlanta: Rodopi, 2001.

Freed, John B. "Bavarian Wine and Woolless Sheep: The *Urbar* of Count Sigiboto IV of Falkenstein (1126–ca. 1198)." *Viator – Medieval and Renaissance Studies* 35 (2004): 71–77.

Freed, John B. *The Counts of Falkenstein: Noble Self-Consciousness in Twelfth-Century Germany*. Philadelphia: American Philosophical Society, 1984.

Freed, John B. *Frederick Barbarossa: The Prince and the Myth*. New Haven: Yale University Press, 2016.

Froning, Richard. *Das Drama des Mittelalters*. 2 vols. Stuttgart: Union Deutsche Verlagsgesellschaft, 1892.

Fuhrmann, Horst. *Germany in the High Middle Ages*. Cambridge: Cambridge University Press, 1986.

Garrison, Mary. "'Send More Socks': On the Mentality and the Preservation Context of Medieval Letters." In *New Approaches to Medieval Communication*, edited by Marco Mostert, 69–99. Turnhout: Brepols, 1999.

Geary, Patrick J. "Land, Language and Memory in Europe 700–1100." *Transactions of the Royal Historical Society* 9 (1999): 169–84.

Georgakopoulou, Alexandra. "Small and Large Identities in Narrative (Inter)Action." In *Discourse and Identity*, edited by Anna De Fina, Deborah Shiffrin, and Michael G. W. Bamberg, 83–102. Cambridge: Cambridge University Press, 2006.

Gilchrist, J. "The Reception of Pope Gregory VII into the Canon Law (1073–1141)." *Zeitschrift der Savigny-Stiftung für Rechtsgeschichte, Kanonistische Abteilung* 90 (August 1973): 35–82.

Godman, Peter. *The Archpoet and Medieval Culture*. Oxford: Oxford University Press, 2014.

Godman, Peter. *The Silent Masters: Latin Literature and Its Censors in the High Middle Ages*. Princeton: Princeton University Press, 2000.

Gundlach, Wilhelm. *Heldenlieder der deutschen Kaiserzeit*. 3 vols. Innsbruck: Verlag der Wagner'schen Universitäts-Buchhandlung, 1899.

Gunter, Günther. *Der Antichrist: Der staufische Ludus de Antichristo*. Hamburg: Friedrich Wittig Publishers, 1970.

Handschin, Jacques. "Conductus-Spicilegien." *Archiv für Musikwissenschaft* 9.2 (1952): 101–19.

Hardison, O. B. *Christian Rite and Christian Drama in the Middle Ages: Essays in the Origin and Early History of Modern Drama*. Baltimore: Johns Hopkins University Press, 1969.

Harvey, David C. "Continuity, Authority and the Place of Heritage in the Medieval World." *Journal of Historical Geography* 26.1 (2000): 47–59.

Hase, Karl. *Das Geistliche Schauspiel*. Leipzig: Breitkopf and Härtel, 1858.
Henning, Lothar, ed. *Die Andechs-Meranier in Franken: Europäisches Fürstentum im Hochmittelalter*. Mainz am Rhein: Philipp von Zabern, 1998.
Hintz, Ernst Ralf. *Learning and Persuasion in the German Middle Ages*. New York: Garland, 1997.
Hoefener, Kristin. "From St. Pinnosa to St. Ursula – The Development of the Cult of Cologne's Virgins in Medieval Liturgical Offices." *The Cult of St. Ursula and the 11,000 Virgins*. Edited by Jane Cartwright. Cardiff: University of Wales Press, 2016.
Holdenried, Anke. *The Sibyl and Her Scribes: Manuscripts and Interpretation of the Latin Sibylla Tiburtina ca. 1050–1500*. New York: Routledge, 2006.
Holladay, Joan A. "The Competition for Saints in Medieval Zurich." *Gesta* 43.1 (2004): 41–59.
Höijer, Birgitta. "Social Representations Theory: A New Theory for Media Research." *Nordicom Review* 32 (2011): 3–16.
Huffman, Joseph Patrick. *The Social Politics of Medieval Diplomacy: Anglo-German Relations (1066–1307)*. Ann Arbor: University of Michigan Press, 2009.
Hughes, Andrew. *Medieval Music: The Sixth Liberal Art*. Toronto: University of Toronto Press, 1980.
Hughes, Kevin L. *Constructing Antichrist*. Washington: Catholic University of America Press, 2005.
Hundt, Friedrich Hector von. *Bayerische Urkunden aus dem XI und XII Jahrhundert*. Munich: K. Akademie, 1878.
Irvine, Martin. *The Making of Textual Culture: 'Grammatica' and Literary Theory, 350–1100*. Cambridge: Cambridge University Press, 1994.
Iversen, Gunilla and Nicolas Bell, eds. *Sapientia et Eloquentia: Meaning and Function in Liturgical Poetry, Music, Drama, and Biblical Commentary in the Middle Ages*. Turnhout: Brepols, 2009.
Izydorczyk, Zbigniew. *Manuscripts of the Evangelium Nicodemi: A Census*. Toronto: Pontifical Institute of Medieval Studies, 1993.
Jackson, W. T. H. "Time and Space in the 'Ludus De Antichristo'." *Germanic Review* 51.1 (Winter 1979): 1–8.
Jaeger, Stephen C. "The Courtier Bishop in vitae from the Tenth to the Twelfth Century." *Speculum* 58.2 (April 1983): 291–325.
Jaeger, Stephen C. *The Envy of Angels: Cathedral Schools and Social Ideals in Medieval Europe, 950–1200*. Philadelphia: University of Pennsylvania Press, 1994.
Jaeger, Stephen C. *The Origins of Courtliness: Civilizing Trends and the Formation of Courtly Ideals 939–1210*. Philadelphia: University of Pennsylvania Press, 1985.
Jaeger, Stephen C. *Scholars and Courtiers: Intellectuals and Society in the Medieval West*. Aldershot: Ashgate, 2002.
Kantorowicz, Ernst H. *The King's Two Bodies: A Study in Mediaeval Political Theology*. Princeton: Princeton University Press, 1957.
Kelly, Henry Ansgar. *Ideas and Forms of Tragedy from Aristotle to the Middle Ages*. Cambridge: Cambridge University Press, 1993.
Kenaan-Kedar, Nurith. "Symbolic Meaning in Crusader Architecture: The Twelfth-Century Dome of the Holy Sepulcher Church in Jerusalem." *Cahiers archéologiques* 23 (1986): 109–17.
Kieckhefer, Richard. *Theology in Stone: Church Architecture from Byzantium to Berkeley*. New York: Oxford University Press, 2004.
Kienzle, Beverly Mayne. "Preaching the Cross: Liturgy and Crusade Propaganda." *Medieval Sermon Studies* 53 (2009): 11–32.
Klaus, Aichele. "The Glorification of Antichrist in the Concluding Scenes of the Medieval 'Ludus De Antichristo'." *Modern Language Notes* 91.3 (April 1976): 424–36.
Kline, Naomi Reed. *Maps of Medieval Thought: The Hereford Paradigm*. Woodbridge: Boydell Press, 2001.

Kobialka, Michal. *This Is My Body: Representational Practices in the Early Middle Ages*. Ann Arbor: University of Michigan, 1999.
Koziol, Geoffrey. *Begging Pardon and Favor: Ritual and Political Order in Early Medieval France*. Ithaca: Cornell University Press, 1992.
Krausen, Edgar, ed. *Die Bistümer der Kirchenprovinz Salzburg. Das Bistum Freising 1. Das Augustinerchorherrenstift Dietramszell*. Germania Sacra Neue Folge 24. Berlin: Walter de Gruyter, 1988.
Kroesen, Justin E. A. "The Altar and its Decorations in Medieval Churches: A Functionalist Approach." *Medievalia* 17 (2014): 153–83.
Kugler, Franciscus. "De Werinhero, sæculi XII. monacho Tegernseensi, et de picturis minutis, quibus carmen suum theotiscum de vita B. V. Mariæ ornavit." Dissertation, University of Berlin, 1831.
Lagueux, Robert C. "Sermons, Exegesis, and Performance: The Laon *Ordo Prophetarum* and the Meaning of Advent." *Comparative Drama* 43.2 (2009): 197–220.
Lampl, Sixtus. *Die Klosterkirche Tegernsee*. Munich: Historischen Vereins von Oberbayern, 1975.
Law, John. "Objects and Space." *Theory, Culture and Society* 19 (2002): 91–105.
Law, John and Kevin Hetherington. "Materialities, Spatialities, and Globalities." *Knowledge, Space, Economy*. Edited by J. R. Bryson. New York: Routledge, 2000.
Leclercq, Jean. *The Love of Learning and the Desire for God: A Study of Monastic Culture*. Translated by Catharine Misrahi. New York: Fordham University Press, 1961.
Lacoste, Debra S. "The Earliest Klosterneuburg Antiphoners." PhD diss., University of Western Ontario, 2000.
Legg, L. G. Wickham. *English Coronation Records*. Westminster: Archibald Constable, 1901.
Long, Micol. "High Medieval Monasteries as Communities of Practice: Approaching Monastic Learning Through Letters." *Journal of Religious History* 41.1 (March 2017): 42–59.
Macy, Gary. *The Theologies of the Eucharist in the Early Scholastic Period: A Study of the Salvific Function of the Sacrament According to the Theologians, ca. 1080–ca. 1220*. Oxford: Clarendon Press, 1984.
Magdalino, Paul. *The Empire of Manuel I Komnenos, 1143–1180*. New York: Cambridge University Press, 1993.
Marchitello, Howard. "Political Maps: The Production of Cartography and Chorography in Early Modern England." *Cultural Artifacts and the Production of Meaning: The Page, the Image, and the Body*. Edited by Margaret J. M. Ezell and Katherine O'Brien O'Keeffe. Ann Arbor: University of Michigan Press, 1994.
Marshall, M. H. "Boethius' Definition of *persona* and Mediaeval Understanding of the Roman Theater." *Speculum* 25 (1950): 471–82.
McGinn, Bernard. *Apocalyptic Spirituality: Treatises and Letter of Lactantius, Adso of Montier-en-Der, Joachim of Fiore, the Spiritual Franciscans, Savonarola*. New York: Paulist Press, 1979.
McGinn, Bernard. *Visions of the End: Apocalyptic Traditions in the Middle Ages*. New York: Columbia University Press, 1979.
McKitterick, Rosamond. *The Carolingians and the Written Word*. Cambridge: Cambridge University Press, 1989.
McKitterick, Rosamond. *History and Memory in the Carolingian World*. Cambridge: Cambridge University Press, 2004.
McLaughlin, Megan. *Sex, Gender, and Episcopal Authority in an Age of Reform, 1000–1122*. Cambridge: Cambridge University Press, 2010.
Melve, Leidulf. *Inventing the Public Sphere: The Public Debate During the Investiture Contest (ca. 1030–1122)*. 2 vols. Leiden: Brill, 2007.
Merriman, Peter. *Mobility, Space and Culture*. New York: Routledge, 2012.
Meuthen, Erich. *Kirche und Heilsgeschichte bei Gerhoh von Reichersberg*. Leiden: Brill, 1959.

Mews, Constant J. "Accusations of Heresy and Error in the Twelfth-Century Schools: The Witness of Gerhoh of Reichersberg and Otto of Freising." In *Heresy in Transition: Transforming Ideas of Heresy in Medieval and Early Modern Europe*, edited by Ian Hunter, John Christian Laursen, and Cary J. Nederman, 43–57. Burlington, Vermont: Ashgate, 2005.

Mews, Constant J. "Monastic Educational Culture Revisited: The Witness of Zwiefalten and the Hirsau Reform." In *Medieval Monastic Education*, edited by George Ferzoco and Carolyn Muessig, 182–98. New York: Leicester University Press, 2000.

Meyer, Wilhelm. "Der Ludus de Antichristo und Bemerkungen über die lateinischen Rhythmen des XII. Jahrhunderts." In *Sitzungsberichte der Philosophisch-Philologischen und Historischen Classe der K.B. Akademie der Wissenschaften zu München*, 1–192. Munich: Akademische Buchdruckerei von F. Straub, 1882.

Michaelis, Eduard. "Zum Ludus de Antichristo." *Zeitschrift für deutsches Altertum und deutsche Literatur* 54.1 (1913): 70–75.

Michaels, Axel. "Zur Dynamik von Ritualkomplexen." *Forum Ritualdynamik* 3 (2003): 6–7.

Miller, Maureen C. *Clothing the Clergy: Virtue and Power in Medieval Europe*. Ithaca: Cornell University Press, 2014.

Miller, Maureen C. "Masculinity, Reform, and Clerical Culture: Narratives of Episcopal Holiness in the Gregorian Era." *Church History* 72 (2003): 25–52.

Miller, Maureen C. *Power and the Holy in the Age of the Investiture Conflict: A Brief History with Documents*. New York: Palgrave MacMillan, 2005.

Mommsen, Theodor Ernst, and Karl Frederick Morrison. *Imperial Lives and Letters of the Eleventh Century*. New York: Columbia University Press, 1962.

Morris, Colin. "Propaganda for War: The Dissemination of the Crusading Ideal in the Twelfth Century." *The Church and War. Studies in Church History* 20 (1983): 79–101.

Moscovici, Serge. *Social Representations: Explorations in Social Psychology*. Edited by Gerard Duveen. New York: New York University Press, 2001.

Müller, Jan-Dirk. "Writing – Speech – Image." In *Visual Culture and the German Middle Ages*, edited by Kathryn Starkey and Horst Wenzel, 35–52. New York: Palgrave Macmillan, 2005.

Munz, Peter. *Frederick Barbarossa: A Study in Medieval Politics*. Ithaca: Cornell University Press, 1969.

Murphy, James J. *Rhetoric in the Middle Ages: A History of Rhetorical Theory from Saint Augustine to the Renaissance*. Los Angeles: University of California Press, 1974.

Myerhoff, Barbara. "The Transformation of Consciousness in Ritual Performances: Some Thoughts and Questions." In *By Means of Performance: Intercultural Studies of Theatre and Ritual*, edited by Richard Schechner and Willa Appel, 245–49. Cambridge: Cambridge University Press, 1990.

Noichl, Elisabeth. *Codex Falkensteinensis: Die Rechtsaufzeichnungen der Grafen von Falkenstein*. Munich: C. H. Beck'sche, 1978.

Noichl, Elisabeth. "Die 'Gründungsurkunde' des Chorherrenstiftes Dietramszell. Eine Tegernseer Fälschung aus dem letzten Viertel des 12. Jahrhunderts."*Archivalische Zeitschrift* (1980): 39–56.

Normington, Katie. *Medieval English Drama*. Cambridge: Polity Press, 2009.

Norton, Michael. *Liturgical Drama and the Reimaging of Medieval Theater*. Kalamazoo: Medieval Institute Publications, 2017.

Norton, Michael J. and Amelia J. Carr. "Liturgical Manuscripts, Liturgical Practice, and the Women of Klosterneuburg." *Traditio* 66 (2011): 67–169.

Novikoff, Alex J. "Anslem, Dialogue, and the Rise of Scholastic Disputation." *Speculum* 86.2 (April 2011): 387–418.

Novikoff, Alex J. *The Medieval Culture of Disputation: Pedagogy, Practice, and Performance*. Philadelphia: University of Pennsylvania Press, 2013.

Nünning, Ansgar and Roy Sommer. "Diegetic and Mimetic Narrativity: Some Further Steps Towards a Narratology of Drama." In *Theorizing Narrativity*, edited by John Pier and Jose Angel Garcia Landa, 331–54. Berlin: Walter de Gruyter, 2008.
Obrist, Barbara. "Wind Diagrams and Medieval Cosmology." *Speculum* 72.1 (January 1997): 33–84.
von Oefele, Edmund. *Geschichte der Grafen von Andechs*. Innsbruck: Wagner'sche Universitäts-Buchhandlung, 1877.
Ogilvy, J. D. A. "*Mimi, Scurrae, Histriones*: Entertainers of the Early Middle Ages." *Speculum* 38.4 (October 1963): 603–19.
Opll, Ferdinand. *Das Itinerar Kaiser Friedrich Barbarossas*. Cologne: Böhlau, 1978.
Pacaut, Marcel. *Frederick Barbarossa*. Translated by A. J. Pomerans. New York: Charles Scribner's Sons, 1970.
Pentcheva, Bissera V. "Hagia Sophia and Multisensory Aesthetics." *Gesta* 50.2 (2011): 93–111.
Petersen, Nils Holger. "Biblical Reception, Representational Ritual, and the Question of 'Liturgical Drama'." In *Sapientia et eloquentia: Meaning and Function in Liturgical Poetry, Music, Drama, and Biblical Commentary in the Middle Ages*, edited by Gunilla Iversen and Nicolas Bell, 163–201. Disputatio 11. Turnhout: Brepols, 2009.
Petersen, Nils Holger. "*Danielis ludus*: Transforming Clerics in the Twelfth Century." *Acta ad archaeologiam et artium historiam pertinentia* 31 (2019): 197–209.
Petersen, Nils Holger. "Liturgical Enactment." In *The Routledge Research Companion to Early Drama and Performance*, edited by Pamela King, 13–29. London: Routledge, 2016.
Petry, Ray C. "Three Medieval Chroniclers: Monastic Historiography and Biblical Eschatology in Hugh of St. Victor, Otto of Freising, and Ordericus Vitalis." *Church History* 34.3 (1965): 282–93.
Pez, Bernhard. *Thesaurus Anecdotorum Novissimus*. 6 vols. Augsburg-Graz: Sumptibus Philippi, Martini, et Joannis Veith Fratrum, 1721.
Pflueger, J. H. L. "On the English Translation of the 'Ludus De Antichristo'." *The Journal of English and Germanic Philology* 44.1 (1945): 24–27.
Pizarro, Joaquín Martínez. *A Rhetoric of the Scene: Dramatic Narrative in the Early Middle Ages*. Toronto: University of Toronto Press, 1989.
Plechl, Helmut. "Die Tegernseer Handschrift Clm 19411: Beschreibung und Inhalt." *Deutsches Archiv für Erforschung des Mittelalters* 18.2 (1962): 418–501.
Plechl, Helmut. "Studien zur Tegernseer Briefsammlung des 12. Jahrhunderts IV, 1." *Deutsches Archiv für Erforschung des Mittelalters* 13.1 (1957): 35–114.
Potter, Robert. *The English Morality Play: Origins, History, and Influence of a Dramatic Tradition*. Boston: Routledge and Kegan Paul, 1975.
Rand, E. K. "Early Mediaeval Commentaries on Terence." *Classical Philology* 4 (1909): 359–89.
Rauh, Horst Dieter. *Das Bild des Antichrist im Mittelalter: Von Tyconius zum deutschen Symbolismus*. Münster: Aschendorff, 1973.
Reeve, Matthew. "Art, Prophecy, and Drama in the Choir of Salisbury Cathedral." *Religion and the Arts* 10.2 (January 2006): 161–90.
Reeves, Marjorie. "The Development of Apocalyptic Thought: Medieval Attitudes." In *The Apocalypse in English Renaissance Thought and Literature*, edited by C. A. Patrides and Joseph Wittreich, 40–72. Manchester: Manchester University Press, 1984.
Reidt, Heinrich. *Das geistliche Schauspiel des Mittelalters in Deutschland*. Frankfurt: Christian Winter, 1868.
Rennie, Kriston R. "Weapons of Reform: Gregory VII, Armenia, and the Liturgy." *Church History* 81.2 (June 2012): 328–47.

Reuschel, Karl. *Die deutschen Weltgerichtsspiele des Mittelalters und der Reformationszeit.* Leipzig: E. Avenarius, 1906.
Reynolds, Roger E. "The Liturgy of Clerical Ordination in Early Medieval Art." *Gesta* 22.1 (1983): 27–38.
Reynolds, Susan. *Kingdoms and Communities in Western Europe, 900–1300.* Oxford: Clarendon Press, 1984.
Rice, Nicole R. "The Feminine Prehistory of the York *Purification*: St. Leonard's Hospital, Civic Drama, and Women's Devotion." *Speculum* 94.3 (July 2019): 704–38.
Richardson, H. G. "The Coronation in Medieval England: The Evolution of the Office and the Oath." *Traditio* 16 (1960): 111–202.
Richardson, Malcolm. "The *Ars dictaminis*, the Formulary, and Medieval Practice." In *Letter-Writing Manuals and Instruction from Antiquity to the Present: Historical and Bibliographic Studies*, edited by Carol Poster and Linda C. Mitchell, 52–66. Columbia: University of South Carolina Press, 2007.
Riedmann, Josef. "Ein neuaufgefundenes Bruchstück des *Ludus de Antichristo*: Beiträge zur Geschichte der Beziehungen zwischen St. Georgenberg in Tirol und Tegernsee." *Zeitschrift für bayerische Landesgeschichte* 36.1 (1973): 16–38.
Robinson, I. S. "The Dissemination of the Letters of Pope Gregory VII During the Investiture Contest." *Journal of Ecclesiastical History* 34.2 (April 1983): 175–93.
Robinson, I. S. *The Papacy, 1073–1198: Continuity and Innovation.* Cambridge: Cambridge University Press, 1990.
Romano, John F. *Liturgy and Society in Early Medieval Rome.* New York: Ashgate, 2014.
Rosenwein, Barbara H. *Emotional Communities in the Early Middle Ages.* Ithaca: Cornell University Press, 2006.
Rosenwein, Barbara H. "Feudal War and Monastic Peace: Cluniac Liturgy as Ritual Aggression." *Viator* 2 (1971): 129–57.
Rowe, Nina. *The Jew, the Cathedral and the Medieval City: Synagoga und Ecclesia in the Thirteenth Century.* New York: Cambridge University Press, 2011.
Rudick, Michael. "Theme, Structure, and Sacred Context in the Benediktbeuern 'Passion' Play." *Speculum* 49.2 (April 1974): 267–86.
Schechner, Richard. *Between Theater and Anthropology.* Philadelphia: University of Pennsylvania Press, 1985.
Schechner, Richard. *The Future of Ritual: Writings on Culture and Performance.* New York: Routledge, 1993.
Schechner, Richard. *Performance Theory.* 2nd edition. London: Routledge, 2003.
Scheer, Monique. "Are Emotions a Kind of Practice (and What Makes them Have a History)? A Bourdieuian Approach to Understanding Emotion." *History and Theory* 51.2 (May 2012): 193–220.
Schein, Sylvia. *Gateway to the Heavenly City: Crusader Jerusalem and the Catholic West (1099–1187).* Burlington: Ashgate, 2005.
Schmeidler, Bernhard. "Über die Tegernseer Briefsammlung (Froumund)." *Neues Archiv der Gesellschaft für Ältere Deutsche Geschichtskunde* 46 (1926): 395–429.
Sciurie, Helga. "Ecclesia und Synagoge an den Domen zu Strassburg, Bamberg, Magdeburg und Erfurt: Körpersprachliche Wandlungen im gestalterischen Kontext." *Wiener Jahrbuch für Kunstgeschichte* 46–47.2 (January 1994): 679–88.
Shepherd, Simon. *Theatre, Body, and Pleasure.* New York: Routledge, 2006.
Silvestri, Angelo. *Power, Politics and Episcopal Authority: The Bishops of Cremona and Lincoln in the Middle Ages (1066–1340).* Newcastle upon Tyne: Cambridge Scholars Publishing, 2015.
Simon, Eckehard, ed. *The Theatre of Medieval Europe: New Research in Early Drama.* Cambridge: Cambridge University Press, 1991.

Sommerville, Robert. *Pope Alexander III and the Council of Tours: A Study of Ecclesiastical Politics and Institutions in the Twelfth Century*. Berkeley: University of California Press, 1977.

Soule, Lesley Wade. *Actor as Anti-character: Dionysus, the Devil, and the Boy Rosalind*. Westport: Greenwood Press, 2000.

Stäblein, Bruno. "Zur Musik des Ludus de Antichristo." In *Zum 70. Geburtstag von Joseph Müller-Blattau*, edited by Christoph-Helmut Mahling, 312–27. Basel: Bärenreiter Kassel, 1966.

Stanzel, F. K. *Linguistische und literarische Aspekte des erzählenden Diskurses*. Vienna: Österreichische Akademie der Wissenschaften, 1984.

Steckel, Sita. *Kulturen des Lehrens im Früh- und Hochmittelalter: Autorität, Wissenskonzepte und Netzwerke von Gelehrten*. Köln: Böhlau, 2011.

Stevens, John. *Words and Music in the Middle Ages: Song, Narrative, Dance and Drama, 1050–1350*. Cambridge: Cambridge University Press, 1986.

Stock, Brian. *The Implication of Literacy: Written Language and Models of Interpretation in the Eleventh and Twelfth Centuries*. Princeton: Princeton University Press, 1983.

Stroll, Mary. *Symbols as Power: The Papacy Following the Investiture Contest*. Leiden: Brill, 1991.

Suydam, Mary A. and Joanna E. Ziegler, eds. *Performance and Transformation: New Approaches to Late Medieval Spirituality*. New York: St. Martin's, 1999.

Symes, Carol. "The Appearance of Early Vernacular Plays: Forms, Functions, and the Future of Medieval Theater." *Speculum* 77.3 (July 2002): 778–831.

Symes, Carol. *A Common Stage: Theater and Public Life in Medieval Arras*. Ithaca: Cornell University Press, 2007.

Symes, Carol. "A Few Odd Visits: Unusual Settings of the *Visitatio sepulchri*." In *Music and Medieval Manuscripts: Paleography and Performance. Essays in Honour of Andrew Hughes*, edited by John Haines and Randall Rosenfeld, 300–22. Aldershot: Ashgate, 2004.

Symes, Carol. "Liturgical Texts and Performance Practices." In *Understanding Medieval Liturgy*, edited by Helen Gittos and Sarah Hamilton, 239–67. Aldershot: Ashgate, 2015.

Symes, Carol. "The Medieval Archive and the History of Theatre." *Theatre Survey* 52.1 (2011): 29–58.

Symes, Carol. "The Performance and Preservation of Medieval Latin Comedy." *European Medieval Drama* 7 (2003): 29–50.

Symes, Carol, ed. and trans. "*Ordo representacionis Ade* (The Play of Adam)." In *The Broadview Anthology of Medieval Drama*, edited by Christina M. Fitzgerald and John T. Sebastian, 23–67. Peterborough: Broadview Press, 2012.

Taylor, Philip M. *Munitions of the Mind: A History of Propaganda*. 3rd edition. Manchester: Manchester University Press, 2003.

Tétreault, Mary Ann. "Formal Politics, Meta-Space, and the Construction of Civil Life." In *Philosophy and Geography II: The Production of Public Space*, edited by Andrew Light and Jonathan M. Smith, 81–98. Lanham: Rowman and Littlefield, 1998.

Thomas, Kyle A. "The *Ludus de Antichristo* and the Making of a Monastic Theatre: Imperial Politics and Performance at the Abbey of Tegernsee 1000–1200." PhD diss., University of Illinois at Urbana-Champaign, 2018.

Thomas, Kyle A. "The Medieval Space: Early Medieval Documents as Stages." *Theatre Survey* 59.1 (January 2018): 4–22.

Thomas, Kyle A. "Playful Performance: Gameplay and Theatre in the Early Middle Ages." *European Medieval Drama* 26 (2022): 185–214.

Thum, Bernd. "Öffentlichkeit und Kommunikation im Mittelalter. Zur Herstellung von Öffentlichkeit im Bezugsfeld elementarer Kommunikationsformen im 13. Jahrhundert." In *Höfische Repräsentation:*

Das Zeremoniell und die Zeichen, edited by Hedda Ragotzky and Horst Wenzel, 65–87. Tübingen: Max Niemeyer Verlag, 1990.

Turner, Cathy and Synne K. Behrndt. *Dramaturgy and Performance*. New York: Palgrave Macmillan, 2008.

Tydeman, William. *The Theatre in the Middle Ages: Western European Stage Conditions, ca. 800–1576*. Cambridge: Cambridge University Press, 1978.

Warning, Rainer. *The Ambivalences of Medieval Religious Drama*. Translated by Steven Rendall. Stanford: Stanford University Press, 2001.

Warning, Rainer and Marshall Brown. "On the Alterity of Medieval Religious Drama." *New Literary History* 10.2 (Winter, 1979): 265–92.

Wells, Scott. "The Warrior *Habitus*: Militant Masculinity and Monasticism in the Henrician Reform Movement." In *Negotiating Clerical Identities: Priests, Monks and Masculinity in the Middle Ages*, edited by Jennifer D. Thibodeaux, 57–85. New York: Palgrave Macmillan, 2010.

Whitbread, Leslie G. "Conrad of Hirsau as Literary Critic." *Speculum* 47.2 (April 1972): 234–45.

Wickham, Glynne. *The Medieval Theatre*. Cambridge: Cambridge University Press, 1974.

Wilks, Michael. "*Apostolicus* and the Bishop of Rome." *The Journal of Theological Studies* 14.2 (October 1963): 314–18.

Winter, Bruce. "The Importance of the 'captatio benevolentiae' in the Speeches of Tertullus and Paul in Acts 24:1–21." *The Journal of Theological Studies* 42.1 (October 1991): 505–31.

Wolff, Luella M. "A Brief History of the Art of Dictamen: Medieval Origins of Business Letter Writing." *The Journal of Business Communication* 16.2 (1979): 3–11.

Wulstan, David. "Liturgical Drama and the 'School of Abelard'." *Comparative Drama* 42.3 (Fall 2008): 347–57.

Young, Karl. *The Drama of the Medieval Church*. 2 vols. Oxford: Clarendon Press, 1933.

von Zezschwitz, Gerhard. *Vom römischen Kaisertum deutscher Nation: Ein mittelalterliches Drama, nebst Untersuchungen über die byzantinischen Quellen der deutschen Kaisersage*. Leipzig: J. C. Hinrichs'sche, 1877.

Ziolkowski, Jan M. "Cultures of Authority in the Long Twelfth-Century." *The Journal of English and Germanic Philology* 108.4 (October 2009): 421–48.

Zysk, Jay. *Shadow and Substance: Eucharistic Controversy and English Drama Across the Reformation Divide*. Notre Dame: University of Notre Dame Press, 2017.

www.ingramcontent.com/pod-product-compliance
Lightning Source LLC
Chambersburg PA
CBHW050123020526
44112CB00035B/2359